INVESTING
WITHOUT
FEAR

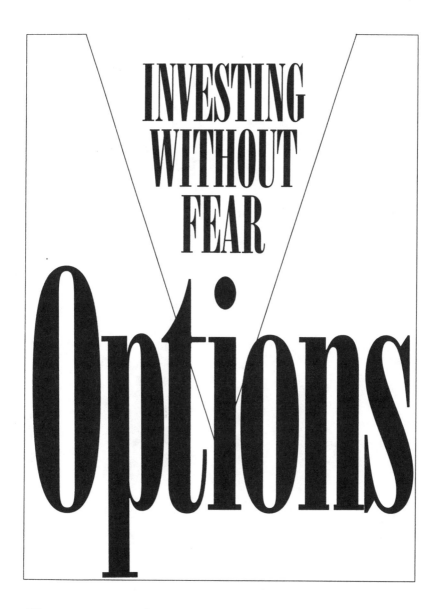

INVESTING WITHOUT FEAR

Options

HARVEY CONRAD FRIEDENTAG

International Publishing Corporation
Chicago, Illinois

International Publishing Corporation
625 N. Michigan Avenue, Suite 1920
Chicago, IL 60611.

Library of Congress Number: 95-75947

ISBN: 0-942641-65-5

Table of Contents

Chapter 3: Options and Potential Returns   31

Chapter 4: Margin–The Credit You Can Use   53

About the Author

The author is a *Registered Investment Adviser* (RIA) with the United States Securities and Exchange Commission and has been managing personal portfolios professionally since 1986. Mr. Friedentag has been certified as a Federal Court expert witness on stock trading; is an acknowledged expert on stock renting, the use of derivatives (exchange-traded equity call options); and serves as President of the Contrarian Investment Club in Denver, Colorado.

Acknowledgements

In *Investing Without Fear—Options*, I have endeavored to write a book that will be useful and valuable to investors. It reflects my involvement over the years with the investment process. More importantly, however, it contains the accumulated knowledge and experience I have gained as a veteran in the stock market.

Writing a book is a formidable task that cannot be appreciated until you actually begin work on it. One must summon forth extraordinary resolve and commitment. One must also draw on the strengths of one's colleagues. Words are inadequate to express my gratitude to Hal and Martha Quiat for their assistance in desktop publishing, grammar, and making me clearly articulate my insights. They were able to divorce their own egos and personalities from the process and concentrate on drawing me out, which they did flawlessly. Behind their gentle exteriors lies a strict discipline: their bold and merciless editing honed the material to the point that only the best of the manuscript made the cut. Hal and Martha's contributions shaped this material. They gave freely of their time and talent, reorganizing their workday to accomodate mine.

Deep thanks are offered to all those who let me interview them, who listened to my long-winded dissertations, and who shared their feelings, philosophies, and experiences about investing.

I have to thank some long-time friends: Stuart MacPhail, for getting me computerized (or I would still be looking at a stack of indecipherable notes), for editing my first drafts, for correcting my grammar, for helping me get my thoughts organized, and for his assistance in getting this book published. Mike Naomi for his constant encouragement, for teaching me computer fundamentals, and for his other efforts on my behalf. Nate Oderberg and Matthew Burns for being there and reviewing my strategies. I am deeply indebted to Thomas Tolen, CPA, for helping me with the tax ramifications of investing, and to Marty Shure, who bounced strategies and ideas off my head and really enhanced my investment procedures.

I have to thank my wife, Beverly, and my family for enduring all the long sessions when I disappeared into my office to work on this book and was thus unavailable to them.

Preface

*"Don't learn the tricks of the trade.
Learn the trade."*
Anonymous

At first glance, the title of this book may seem to be a contradiction. Aren't investors by definition fearful? Those with little training in investing tend to do nothing, or they delegate investment responsibilities to others (stockbrokers, accountants, bank trust officers, insurance agents, relatives, friends, etc.), often with disappointing results. After all, no one will care as much about your financial assets as you do. No one will do the job as well as you can.

It is not an easy job. There are thousands of ways to go wrong. Even the most prudent investment decisions may not work (as we know from personal experiences and the tales of countless investors). The job may not be easy, but *is* doable—you *can* learn to invest money successfully. It takes some study and considerable personal discipline, but you will be well rewarded for your efforts. This book will help guide you toward profitable accomplishments.

Investing Without Fear—Options is not for beginners. It is for investors who have been unsuccessful in buying stocks, who have either made small gains or, worse, lost money. The strategies discussed herein use tactics designed for the 1990s and, once learned, they are easy to execute. They will allow you to accumulate assets steadily, so that you can reach your investment goals within a reasonable amount of time.

The book begins by reviewing briefly the worst day of fear ever known by investors—the Stock Market Crash of 1929—and illustrates how the lessons of the past can teach you how to invest fearlessly. Later chapters will teach you how to make profits when the market moves up, down, or sideways.

An abundance of books is available about the stock market. I encourage you to read and study those listed in the Bibliography. There is no one book that is perfect for all investors, as their experience, goals, philosophies, and capital vary greatly. I trust, however, that *Investing Without Fear—Options* will be welcomed by many.

CHAPTER 1

Fear and Ignorance

"Fear always springs from ignorance."
Ralph Waldo Emerson

Today a growing number of people are entranced with the subject of investing, without having acquired any basic know-how. Most become amateur investors; many find themselves caught in a poor deal, afraid to invest again; few become successful.

Making the leap from serious to successful investor, while seemingly a simple and evolutionary step, is quite complex. The desire to become a successful investor can be strong, but with it comes the task of developing an investment strategy. It is how you pursue your interest that usually sparks the jump from casual investor to successful status. Even if you are not going to become a professional investor, you have to think and invest like one.

No matter what the strategy, stock selection demands fundamental knowledge. What you see today in the economy of our country and the stock market has happened before and will occur again. You can learn the fundamentals by understanding some stock market economic conditions and their meanings.

Stock cycle is a period of expansion (recovery) and contraction (recession) in economic activity, which affects inflation, growth, employment, and prices of stocks.

△ *Bull market* is a period of prolonged rise in the prices of stocks, bonds, or commodities. Bull markets usually last a few months and are characterized by high trading volume. △ *Bear market* is a prolonged period of falling prices. A bear market in stocks is usually brought on by the anticipation of declining economic activity.

> *"The best part of the future is the past."*
> Chinese Proverb

Lessons from History

In the short 200-year history of U.S. securities trading, a series of important stock market bottoms appear in a 60-year stock cycle pattern—1800, 1860, 1920, and 1980. What makes the cycle pertinent? Each bull market that followed these bottoms was followed, in turn, by a significant bear market collapse about a decade later.

The 1929-1932 Market Crash

The most dramatic market setback was the 1929-1932 Crash, which saw the Dow drop nearly 90%. Here's what happened.

Tuesday, October 29, 1929: Stocks dropped $10, to $70. Shortly after 8 a.m. on Tuesday, October 29, 1929, prices were down 1 to 50 points on both the big board and the curb exchange. During the day slight recoveries set in, but these were without support, and the stocks which had recovered fell back. At 2:10 p.m. 13,838,000 shares had changed hands. At this time, the stock ticker tape was 82 minutes late. There was a mid-afternoon rally from the lows, which brought prices back from the minimums but still left them down enormously on the day.

Wednesday October 30, 1929: Stocks advanced $5, to $30. Investment trusts and trading corporations were heavy buyers of stock on both Tuesday and Wednesday. Estimates of these purchases ranged from $350 million to one-half billion dollars. On Wednesday, the bulls staged a great demonstration in the closing minutes. Prices were whirled up to the highs of the day, a day that had seen prices moving up regularly from their lows of Tuesday.

The nation's leading financial forces mobilized to calm the wave of hysteria and restore confidence in the securities markets. John D. Rockefeller, Sr., and his son announced that, for some days, they had been purchasing sound common stocks. Julius Rosenwald, philanthropist and chairman of the board of Sears, Roebuck and Company, "pledged, without limit" his personal fortune to guarantee the stock market accounts of the 40,000 employees of his company (a plan he had also adopted during the depression in 1921).

Thursday, October 31, 1929: The three-hour stock exchange session on Thursday saw traders push the market forward at such a pace that 10 billion dollars was added to the market's valuation of stock, and profit taking failed to wipe out the gains. The first half-hour alone was at a rate of more than 24 million shares. Tickers ran an hour behind, but floor quotations at closing time showed stocks were up from 1 to 40 points. Buying was as frenzied on Thursday as selling had been on Tuesday. Values came back with the vigor of the old bull market that Wall Street had declared dead a few days ago.

The following comparison illustrates that a lot of money would have been made as a result of the 1929-32 Market Crash:

Dow Jones

October 29, 1929 -30.57; Percent Change -11.73%
October 30, 1929 +28.40; Percent Change +12.34%

Financial hell or financial heaven may be just around the corner. However, a prepared investor can profit when the market goes up *or* down. It's best to emulate investors like John D. Rockefeller, Sr., and Julius Rosenwald.

Market Madness: Black Monday, October 19, 1987

This stock market crash sent the Dow Jones Industrial Average (DJIA) plummeting 508 points, to 1,738.74, and total market losses climbed to more than half a trillion dollars. In heavy trading the market Dow closed down 77.42 points, at 1,950.43, on Thursday, October 22, 1987.

Among the issues most heavily traded was IBM. On Tuesday, trading in the stock was halted to stop the flow of panic selling. Several other companies reacted to the debacle by buying back large portions of their shares at discounted prices in order to show confidence in their future and discourage takeovers.

If you had bought IBM stock on Monday, October 19, you would have profited in just two days, as shown in the following table.

Company	Oct. 19	Oct. 21	Net Gain
IBM	103 1/4	122 3/4	19.50
AT&T	23 5/8	29 1/2	5.87
Bell South	33 3/4	39 1/2	5.75

While almost no company's stock escaped unscathed, the utilities did not get hit as hard as others. Utilities are considered to be safe, or defensive stocks.

Again, a comparison reveals that a lot of money could have been made in just two days:

Dow Jones
October 19, 1987 -508; Percent Change -22.61%
October 21, 1987 +186; Percent Change +10.15%

At least part of Black Monday's market bedlam was attributed to computer trading by institutional investors who preprogram their computers to buy or sell stocks at a predetermined price.

After the 1987 crash, circuit breakers were installed to prevent large-scale, rapid, one-day market swings. Today we also have the Federal Reserve System poised to head off any starting panic. A large service sector now exists that is less exposed to swings in the economic cycle. Finally, increased government spending and social programs serve as shock absorbers to jolts in the general economy.

Alas, these two historical examples show that human nature never changes. Fear follows greed as surely as night follows day. This is what creates cycles. What they say is so: "Those who don't learn from the past are bound to repeat it."

What Causes Stock Market Anxiety?

When the DJIA is near its all-time high, luring speculators into the market, the "buy now before it goes up further" mentality is prevalent. When this occurs, other factors in the economy are affected as well.

When inflation is very high, it destroys the integrity of the dollar and dollar-sensitive investments. Inflation causes people to lose confidence in the currency and put their assets in real estate or gold.

When interest rates are very high, the cost of using money will be high. Business expansion will be curtailed and consumer spending will go down.

When inflation is low, growth in the U.S. economy will be low, affecting consumer spending and confidence. This will result in fewer job opportunities as companies cut back, lowering production and services.

When fear of recession (and possibly a depression) is growing, the effect is falling prices, reduced purchasing, rising unemployment, increased inventories, deflation, and factory closings. When business and personal debt are costly, more people will default on their loans in spite of the obligation and liability to repay. Corporate and personal taxes will be very high, causing the real return on investment and disposable income to go down.

When the size of government and its spending is very high, it causes taxes to rise, making a new spiral upwards in inflation, and makes prices go up affecting our export business.

When business and savings are low, consumer confidence falls. The money available for investment is scarce, which makes interest rates rise.

When uncertainties are growing, such as threats of war, OPEC oil price increases, threats to our industries by foreign competition, pollution, and waste disposal, there will be growth in unemployment, minority unrest, social insecurity, and crime.

During times of market anxiety there will be:

- a probable drop in stock prices;
- low incentive to invest in common stock; and
- low reward-to-risk ratios.

During times of market euphoria there will be:

- a probable rise in stock prices;
- high incentive to invest in common stock; and
- high reward-to-risk ratios.

There are two ways to learn anything—the hard way through harsh experience, or the comfortable way by studying. Success in the stock market is dependent on acquiring adequate knowledge and then utilizing it with confidence.

Rules to Invest By

The antidote to market anxiety and euphoria are principles that I have studied and embraced. My stock market insights follow.

1. Always do your research.
2. Always be fully invested in equities.
3. Always have patience and discipline: 95% of the market moves are unpredictable and perhaps 5% are predictable.
4. Always maximize the time value of your money. Remember compounding.
5. Always buy stock at or below the average of the years' high and low price.
6. Always take your profit when the stock is overvalued.
7. Always reinvest your dividends and capital gains.
8. Always have your money actively working for you producing after tax returns greater than current inflation.
9. Always disregard "hot tips."
10. Always avoid the "madness of crowds" or the herd instinct prevailing in the stock market.
11. Always balance momentum, growth, and value.
12. Always use a discount broker. Trades are easy and fast and commission discounts can make the difference between profit and loss.
13. Never buy stocks at market; make them limit orders.
14. Never have money sitting around doing nothing or loafing—earning some return but not keeping up with inflation after taxes.
15. Never buy the sympathy stock. Never buy a weak company because a strong one has started to move. Many do this, and it is rarely profitable. Buy the company that is going up.
16. Never marry a stock.
17. Never buy a stock that did not go up in a bull market. "Smart money" is never placed on a nonachiever.
18. Never sell a stock that did not go down in a bear market. The "smart money" is holding its position.

19. Never sell an inactive stock just as it begins to move up.
20. Never overpay for comfort, excitement, and appeal. This is a trap for uninformed investors.

In the rest of the book, I offer a simple approach to an investment method that has served me well for 17 years of professional investing. The techniques, strategies, and attitudes are presented. There have been boom times and also the great Crash of 1987, and my procedures worked through both. Only those who are willing to exercise the necessary discipline and patience required by my investing philosophy will be able to successfully invest without fear in options.

CHAPTER 2

Options and the Stock Market

"Money is a sixth sense which makes it possible for us to enjoy the other five."
Richard Ney

You are now ready to be introduced to the real world of the stock market. A stock can do three things: go up, go down, or stay the same in value. Regardless what the stock value does, it can be to your advantage. You will learn how to deal with this characteristic, *volatility*, and make money. You will also learn about the brokerage industry's wonder weapon: exchange-listed options.

What Is An Option?

Option: 1. to wish, desire. 2. . . . choosing; choice. 3. the power, right, or liberty of choosing. 4. the right, acquired for a consideration, to buy or sell . . . something at a fixed price . . . within a specified time.
Webster's New World Dictionary

These definitions apply perfectly to options in the stock market.

An option is a legal contract which gives the holder the right to buy or sell a specified stock at a specified price—the *strike price*—before a specified date—the *expiration date*.

An option contract to purchase stock is a *call* and an option contract to sell stock is a *put*. A call or a put represents 100 shares of stock.

Listed options are securities that are regulated by the exchange on which they are traded. A listed securities option is a contract to buy or sell units of an underlying security at a specified price, at any time before the option expires. An option contract is for 100 shares (unless adjusted for stock splits or stock dividends).

Option buyers, or holders, pay a premium for the right to buy or sell the underlying security. The seller, or writer, of a call option is obligated to sell the underlying security to the option buyer if the call is exercised. The seller, or writer, of a put option is obligated to buy the underlying stock if the put is exercised.

The essential elements of an option contract are the *strike price*, *premium*, and *expiration date*.

The strike price, or exercise price, is the price at which the underlying security can be bought or sold. The premium is the price the buyer pays in return for the rights conveyed in the option.

The *expiration date* is the last day on which the option can be exercised.

Options and Common Stocks

Options share many similarities with common stocks. Both are listed securities. Orders to buy and sell options are handled through brokers in the same way as orders to buy and sell stocks. Listed option orders are executed on the trading floors of national Securities and Exchange Commission (SEC)-regulated exchanges where all trading is conducted in an open, competitive auction market.

Like stocks, options trade with buyers making bids and sellers making offers. In stocks, those bids and offers are for shares of stock. In options, the bids and offers are for the right to buy or sell 100 shares (per option contract) of the underlying stock at a given price per share for a given period of time.

History of Options

In the year 1694, put and call options were introduced in London, England. Three centuries later put and call options continue to be an important element of security dealings.

Introduced into this country about a century ago, they soon became the favorite speculative tool of the old-time Wolves of Wall Street. The conventional shied way from them, and many to this day cast a prejudiced eye upon options. The ordinary investor used to regard dealing in puts and call as a special, complicated maneuver, tinged with evil. About 40 years ago, when threatened with the elimination of option trading, the Put and Call Brokers and Dealers Association instituted rules and standards that resulted in a degree of respectability for put and call options. Since then, stock options have become better understood, and more widely used by investors to hedge against price movements, to protect unrealized profits, and for potential tax savings.

Although the history of options extends over centuries, it was not until 1973 that standardized, exchange-listed, and government-regulated options became available. In only a few years, these options almost displaced the limited trading in over-the-counter options. Option trading has become an indispensable tool for the securities industry.

Function of the Options Clearing Corporation

Standardized option contracts provide orderly, efficient, and liquid option markets.

Options are an extremely versatile investment tool. Because of their unique risk/reward structure, options can be used with other financial instruments to create a hedged position. Unlike other investments where the risk may have no limit, options offer a known risk to buyers.

The Options Clearing Corporation (OCC) selects the companies to be listed on the option exchanges. Though most companies favor this listing because it adds interest in their securities, the choice is not theirs. Listing requirements state that trading of the company stock must be at a high volume and above $10 per share. If these requirements are not met, new option expirations are not traded, and when existing contracts expire companies are delisted.

The OCC guarantees that the terms of an option contract will be honored. There are no ifs, ands, or buts with options.

Before the existence of option exchanges and the OCC, an optionholder who wanted to exercise an option depended on the ethical and financial integrity of the writer or his brokerage firm for performance. Also, there was no convenient means of closing-out one's position before the expiration of the contract. The OCC, as the common clearing entity for all SEC-regulated option transactions, resolves these difficulties. Once OCC is satisfied that there are matching orders from a buyer and a seller, it severs the link between the parties. In effect, the OCC becomes the buyer to the seller and the seller to the buyer, guaranteeing contract performance. The seller can buy back the same option he has written, closing-out the transaction and terminating his obligation to deliver the underlying stock. This in no way affects the right of the original buyer to sell, hold, or exercise his option. All premium and settlement payments are made to and paid by the OCC.

Option Valuation

The price or premium of an option is dependent on the:

1. difference between the current stock price and the strike price;

2. period of time to expiration of the option (more time costs more money); and
3. price movement (volatility) of the underlying stock.

The underlying security is the stock which can be purchased or sold according to the terms of the option contract and is the base upon which a sound option-writing program rests. Volatility is a measure of stock price fluctuations. The ideal stock for option writing would be one with medium volatility and a growth potential based on solid fundamental value. A divided is also preferable, but not a requirement.

Option Valuation Example

ABC Corp. stock is selling on the New York Stock Exchange (NYSE) at $32 a share today.

Choice One gives the buyer the right to buy ABC Corp. stock at $25 a share.

Choice Two gives the buyer the right to buy ABC Corp. stock at $35 a share.

Choice One is more valuable, since the buyer would rather have an option to pay $25 for a $32 stock. As a result, it costs more to buy Choice One than to buy Choice Two.

Sellers know this, so as the stock price rises and falls, the option price rises and falls with it. As time elapses towards the expiration date the option price falls because of the wasting time value. Option investors, like stock investors, can follow price movements, trading volume, and other pertinent information day-by-day or even minute-by-minute.

However, there are some important differences between options and common stocks that should be noted. Unlike common stock, an option has a limited life. Common stocks can be held indefinitely in the hope that their value may increase, while an option has an expiration date. If an option is not closed out or exercised before its expiration date, it ceases to exist as a financial instrument. Thus, an option is considered a "wasting asset."

There is not a fixed number of options, as there is with common stock shares. An option is simply a contract involving a buyer willing to pay a price to obtain certain rights and a seller willing to grant these rights in return for the price. Thus, the number of outstanding option contracts, commonly called "open interest," depends solely on the number of buyers and sellers interested in receiving and giving these rights.

Unlike stocks that have certificates, option positions are shown on printed statements prepared by a buyer's or seller's brokerage firm. This procedure sharply reduces paperwork and delays.

Finally, while stock ownership gives the holder a share of the company, including certain voting rights and rights to dividends (if any), the option owner's only benefit is from an upward price movement of the stock.

The Option Contract

The *option contract* is defined by the following elements: type (a call or a put), underlying security (deliverable security), strike price, and expiration date. All option contracts that are the same type, cover the same underlying security, and have the same strike price and same expiration date, are referred to as an *option series* and are fungible.

Fungibility is a very important word for option traders. All fungible assets such as commodities, options, and securities are interchangeable. For example, an investor's shares of ABC Corp. left in custody at a brokerage firm are freely mixed with other shares of ABC Corp. Likewise, stock options are freely interchangeable among investors, just as wheat stored in a grain elevator is not specifically identified as to its ownership. (We will later show how to use fungibility to our advantage.)

The Option Premium

The option premium is the cash price exchanged when buying or selling options. Premiums fluctuate depending on the duration of the contract, the strike price, and the current price of the underlying stock. Premiums can run as high as 25% of the value of the underlying stocks. For example, for a volatile stock selling at 20 ($2,000 for 100 shares), the premium for a call to be exercised in 9 months might be 5 ($500) when the exercise price is also 20.

Shorter-term options on more stable stocks carry smaller premiums, from 2% for expiration in a month to 10% for those with longer maturities. However, additional commission costs will cut returns on these shorter-term options.

The writer of an option is obligated to deliver the underlying security if the option is exercised. Whether or not an option is ever exercised, the writer keeps the premium.

Premiums are quoted on a per-share basis. Thus, a premium of 1 represents a premium payment of $100 per option contract ($1.00 × 100 shares). Premium quotations are stated in points and fractions.

An option buyer cannot lose more than the price of the option premium paid. The option will expire as worthless if the conditions for profitable exercise do not occur by the expiration date. Remember, options are wasting assets which go to zero with time.

In a stock option contract the premium is the only variable. The number of shares, the expiration month, and the strike prices are all standardized.

Option Strategy

To some investors, the very mention of the word "option" evokes images of very speculative, highly leveraged trades. However, there is an option strategy that is quite conservative and appropriate for most equity investors.

Most people are aware of only one side of options, the side that is frequently advertised on financial television. The advertisements state that "buying an option on stock offers the chance for unlimited profit with a limited risk." Buying options are like buying lottery tickets—you could win big, but the odds are against winning at all.

If buying options is a risky endeavor, how about selling them?

Selling options is not risky and you win small, but often. The money-makers in options trading are those who sell them; their winnings are never spectacular, just regular.

The strategy I referred to above is *covered call writing*. The covered call writer either:

a. buys stock and simultaneously sells an equivalent number of call options (buy-write); or
b. sells call with stock that is already owned.

The benefits of this strategy are three-fold:

1. It places money in the investor's account.
2. It increases the investor's probability of profit, often substantially.
3. It allows investors to make a profit, sometimes 50 to 80% annualized, and not worry about the swings of stock prices.

Covered Call Options

A *covered call option* is sold by an investor owning the underlying stock. In case the option is exercised, the seller is covered by the stock that is owned. For example, an investor who holds 100 shares of AT&T common is considered "covered" if he writes one option on his stock.

From now on we will refer to covered call options simply as options. Keep in mind though that they represent a powerful, mysterious segment of the financial market.

We shall be studying call options, the most popular and widely used option. We will not be using put options, which are the mirror image of call options. Calls are for the right to buy stocks; puts are for the right to sell stocks.

Using exchange-listed options enhances returns in a variety of ways:

- by hedging downside risk;
- by combining risk protection with upside potential;
- by making tactical adjustments without having to buy or sell securities; and
- by increasing liquidity through more risk/reward alternatives.

What Is a Covered Writer?

A *covered writer* is the seller, or writer, of an option contract who owns the underlying stock. Option writers are normally conservative investors seeking additional current income.

Before we go any further, let's understand the first important point. We will always be selling, which means we will always be taking in money. The buyer is on the risky side. He has to predetermine the value of the stock and the time period he wants. The buyer is always paying, which means he is giving money away. We are always going to be taking in money—nice, yes?

Sophisticated traders use complex combination spreads, strips, straps, and straddles. We shall not be discussing these at all, as they do not figure into our philosophy of investing without fear.

It is our intention always to be selling covered call options, making us the covered option writer. We are not concerned with the other techniques that are available in the option market. We will be using one strategy, *i.e.,* buying an *optionable stock* and writing covered call options on that stock. An optionable stock is one listed on an option exchange (comprising approximately 1,500 companies).

Ninety percent of my investing involves the stocks of high-quality companies. Ten percent is done in slightly higher-risk companies with the potential of higher rewards. All my investing is done in covered call writing. I should add that 75% of my gains result from dealing in options.

I am conservative. As the saying goes, I am concerned less with the return on my money than I am with the return of my money. I wish to stress that neither I nor anyone else knows for sure if a stock is going to go up or down. I do know the prices at which I am a happy buyer or a happy seller. If the stocks do nothing I will be getting more than the return of a money market investment. Options allow me to own stock in a more conservative manner. Instead of trying for the big capital gain, I can get a good return, with some participation on the upside, through covered call options. I know what the rates of return will be if the stock is called away or if it stays unchanged through expiration. If the stock goes down, the option premium offers some cushion. The key is discipline, which I shall stress over and over.

> *"Discipline fortifies the heart with virtuous principles, enlightens the mind with useful knowledge, and furnishes it with enjoyment from within itself."*
> Hugh Blair

At-, In-, and Out-of-the-Money

Understanding the fundamentals of covered option writing is essential to learning how to distinguish a good covered write. When you write (sell) options, you start with an immediate, sure, limited profit rather than the potential for a greater, but uncertain, gain. The most you can make is the premium you receive even if the price of the stock soars. When you write options on the stock you own, any loss of the value of the stock will be reduced by the amount of the premium received.

The strike price for an option is initially set at a price that is close to the current share price of the underlying security. Additional or subsequent strike prices are set at the following intervals: 2½ points when the strike price to be set is $25 or less, 5 points when the strike price is over $25. New strike prices begin when the price of the underlying security rises to the highest, or falls to the lowest, strike price currently available. If the strike price of an option is less than the current market price of the underlying security, the option is said to be *in-the-money*. The holder of this option has the right to buy the stock at a price that is less than the current market price. If the strike price of an option is more than the stock price, it is said to be *out-of-the-money*. If the strike price equals the current market price, the option is said to be *at-the-money*. Examples of each follow.

At-the-Money Options

These are written at an exercise price that is at or close to the current price of the stock.

In January, Paul Prudent buys 100 shares of Always Good (AG) at 20 and sells a July option, at the strike price of 20, for $2 ($200). Paul realizes that AG may move above $22 in the next 6 months but is willing to accept the $2 per share income.

John, the option buyer, anticipating that AG will move up well above $22, got the right to buy the stock for $20 anytime before the expiration date in July.

Paul will not realize a dollar loss until the price of AG goes below $18. At $22 the profit starts for John, the option buyer. Let's see what happens if AG stock rises to $30. Anytime before expiration in July, John can exercise his option and pay $2,000 for stock then worth $3,000. After deducting about $300 (the $200 premium plus commissions), John will have a net profit of about $700.

If the price of AG stock moves up to only $22, John will call (exercise the option) and buy the stock, but will not be even because of the premium and commission costs. Paul would have sold the AG stock for $22 ($20 for the stock and $2 for the option), plus two dividends of $25 each.

If the price of AG stock stays at $20, Paul will still own the stock, keep the $200 premium, and can write a new option.

In-the-Money Options

This is a more aggressive technique that requires more attention, but can result in great profits and tax benefits.

In January, Joe Smart buys 300 shares of Fantastic Furs (FF) at $20 ($6,000) and sells three July 15 options at $7 each ($2,100). If FF stock stays at or below 15, Joe keeps the premiums and the stock. If it goes to 25, he can buy back the options for $10 (stock price $25 - strike price $15 = $10), or a total price of $3,000 ($10 × 300) to set up a short-term tax loss of - $900 ($3,000 buyback - $2,100 option money = -$900) Joe can sell the shares for $7,500 ($25 per share × 300 shares = $7,500), for a $1,500 gain ($7,500 sale price - $6,000 cost) $900 option loss, a net gain of $600.

If FF stock drops below 15, Joe keeps the premiums and writes new options. He won't suffer a loss, until his real cost of $13 ($20 stock cost - $7 option premium) drops below $13.

In-the-money options are sold at strike prices below the current price of the stock. Since the options involve a smaller investment, there is a higher percentage of return and, in a down market, more protection from loss. In the above example Joe started with $6,000 worth of stock with an actual cash outlay of $3,900, because of the option premium received.

Out-of-the-Money Options

These are written at an exercise price that is above the current price of the stock.

In this example Sally Surething owned 300 shares of Safest Safes Industries (SSI) which she had bought at $10 two years earlier. Sally, anticipating a rise in the stock price, wrote an option at a higher strike price. In January, when SSI was at $20, she wrote three option contracts for July 25 at $3 ($900 premiums $3 × 300 = $900). In July SSI was at 26 and she was exercised. Sally received $25 for the stock and had received a $3 premium, for a total sale price of $28 when the stock was only $26.

Out-of-the-money options work best in an up market with quality stocks that are bought when undervalued and when there are far-out options (6-9 months) with a rich premium. Of course, if the stock price was below $25 at expiration, the option owner would not exercise his rights and Sally could rewrite the options again for an additional premium.

Option Exercise

The option holder buys the underlying stock from the option writer. If the holder of a call option decides to exercise his right, he must notify his broker. The brokerage firm, upon receiving an exercise notice, will assign one or more of its customers, either randomly or on a first-in, first-out basis. They may assign the total to one seller. They may assign parts of several sellers' contract to fulfill their obligation. This results in multiple commissions for the brokerage firm, and you should object strongly if this occurs. The assigned writer is obligated to sell the underlying shares of stock at the specified strike price.

Option Fundamentals

The *cash premium* equals the sum of the *time value* and the *intrinsic value*. It is received from the sale of the call, which effectively reduces the cost of buying the stock (not the cost basis), providing a measure of downside protection for the investor against declines in the stock price. The premium effectively increases the yield on the investor's position.

Time value represents the value of the time remaining to expiration of the option. Generally, investors want to sell calls with as much time value as possible. Time value is the part of an option's total price that exceeds intrinsic value. If the option has no intrinsic value, it consists entirely of time value. In general, the greater time value on a covered write, the better the downside protection and the higher the total return will be.

Intrinsic value is the in-the-money portion of an option's price (the difference between the exercise price or strike price of an option and the market value of the underlying security).

The most important consideration when developing a covered write option strategy is the underlying stock. The investor must have a positive opinion on the stock. I look for stocks with solid value; I do not second-guess the market to find a stock that is going to be a big gainer.

The second consideration must be the rate of return generated by the position. The combined return from the appreciation on the stock, the option premium, and the dividends received should exceed alternative investments with comparable risk/reward characteristics.

This is a conservative investment approach. The idea behind it is to earn added income from assets that are solid and productive in their own right. The stock selection process used is a defensive one. Stocks chosen are those that pay a good option premium. The emphasis in this approach is *not losing*.

By following a rigid discipline, we overcome many amateur errors. There is absolutely no room for the latest "hot tip" or "gut feeling." To repeat, the most important part of the investment program is the quality of the underlying security.

The stocks included in your options program should be evaluated using dividend yields, price/earnings (PE) ratio, and the stock's market history. The stocks in your portfolio will be chosen because they are optionable and because they pay a high premium.

The successful investor diversifies his stock holdings as much as possible. Normally, the more stocks in the portfolio, the lower the risk.

Investing without fear requires the following steps:

1. Buy a carefully selected stock.
2. Sell options (collect a premium).
3. When an option expires, write another option (collect a premium).
4. When an option is exercised, the stock is assigned and sold for the strike price.

The goal of option writing is to reduce risk and to generate extra income. The March 1986 *Changing Times* (now called *Kiplinger's Personal Finance Magazine*) says, "After wincing over single-digit returns, it's no wonder that interest-starved investors perk up at talk of squeezing extra yield from their stocks." This extra yield is after commissions and on top of dividends paid by the stock.

The fascinating question is, why would someone be willing to give you extra profit? The answer is that there are really two "someones" involved.

The most visible "someone" is the brokerage firm offering the chance for riches by enticing investors to buy options. The firm is willing to offer the chance for unlimited wealth because it gets a commission to act as broker.

The other "someone" is the seller of the option. Most sellers are professional traders, both on and off the exchange trading floor. They are willing to sell options for the same reasons as insurance companies and mutual funds: in order to increase their earnings and have a protective hedge against a downside in the market. They are familiar with the markets; they know that the market will move and they can balance potential risk against potential reward.

There are always opportunities for individual investors to use options as a part of a total plan. With careful selections and constant monitoring, selling options can boost annual income by 15% or more; can be used for tax benefits and low costs (small commissions compared to those of stocks); and can offer a variety of choice (in underlying assets, strike prices, and time frames).

Remember! Never buy options, sell them!
Buying options is speculation! Selling options is investing!

The Option Advantage

Every dollar that option buyers lose goes into the pockets of option sellers. Since a majority of options expire worthless, it means that the seller of an option who waits for it to expire has a good chance of making a profit. Investors with adequate time and the financial resources to operate on the seller's side of the options market can build a fortune with these odds.

	Stocks	Covered Calls & Stocks	Buy Options
Leverage	1 to 1	1.1 to 1	10 to 1
Minimum Cost	100%	90%	5%
Maximum Loss	Limit of Investment	Limit of Investment	Limit of Investment
Risk	Low	Lowest	Highest

Selling (or writing) options turns off most uninformed investors. One reason is that there doesn't seem to be much money in it. Most stock option transactions sell for $500 or less. Assuming the option expires totally worthless, the option writer can't earn more than the premium received for the option. Option writing doesn't deliver the instant returns of 200 or 300% possible when buying options.

However, the probability is that over the long term, the option writer will make far bigger profits than will the speculator who buys options in hopes of making a quick killing. In the options market, the writers of options have 85 to 90% odds in their favor. It is the time premium that tips the odds in favor of the option seller.

While buying options offers the promise and occasionally the reality of big profits, selling options is the wonder weapon that holds the potential for getting "interest-free loans," avoiding the concerns of price swings in the stock market, and getting a 25 to 40% annualized yield. Selling options puts money into the investor's account.

Why is something this good kept almost a secret? Because it is more complicated than merely buying and holding stocks, and most brokers do not really understand the full potential.

There are many individual investors who want to sell options and reap the benefits. Since the option seller is selling time value, he can frequently make money whether the market stays the same, goes up, or goes down, increasing the probability of profit and enabling him to reap the benefits of investing without fear.

Using Margin

"You cannot discover new oceans unless you have the courage to lose sight of the shore."

Anonymous

With my options method you will:

1. sell covered call options to hedge your position and make profits with possible tax advantages; and
2. use *margin* to enhance your portfolio and ease your taxes.

What? A book entitled *Investing Without Fear—Options* advocating dangerous methods?

Options? That is gambling.

Margin? That is borrowing.

You are suggesting that I borrow to gamble!

Even some of Wall Street's savvy investors recoil at the mention of options. Others will tell you of the poor performance of the mutual funds that used options in their strategy. "If the pros can't do it, you can't do it." Yet the realm of puts and calls isn't reserved solely for speculators with ice in their veins. Options can be a part of a very conservative hedging strategy. You will know why the option funds do not do well when you understand the correct method of selling options.

Still others will tell you that the stock market is dangerous enough, and it is no place to use borrowed funds to invest. It is important to understand the meaning of margin. The rational use of margin need be no more risky than buying a house with a mortgage.

The ideas about options and margin are the most prevalent misconceptions in the stock market. I will teach you to understand the use of options and margin, what can be done with them, what mistakes to avoid, and how to protect yourself against their misuse (thus avoiding the consequences).

Options and margin can be effective tools for enhancing total return of an undervalued, diversified, long-term stock portfolio. Not many stock market participants (investors, stockbrokers, bankers, lawyers, and accountants) really understand all the technicalities of margined and optioned portfolios, especially the underlying rational assumptions.

What is Margin?

Margin is the amount a customer deposits with a broker when borrowing from the broker to buy securities. A brokerage account which permits an investor to purchase securities on credit and to borrow on securities already in the account is a *margin account*. Buying on credit and borrowing funds for the period that the loan is outstanding.

Using margin can increase the percentage of profit on your investment by a surprisingly large amount, as it allows you to hold a larger portfolio and take advantage of downturns in the market to buy bargains. The cost of borrowing on margin is very low. Within certain limits, margin loan interest can be tax-deductible, as well.

A margin loan against the value of your portfolio is limited to 50%. Since it is open-ended, there are no monthly payments. Interest is deducted from your account monthly. Which is safer, a home loan made with 10% down or a margin loan made with 50% down? You can take out too large a mortgage, experience an economic downturn, or have a run of bad luck. Under such circumstances, you would lose your home or car by defaulting on your monthly payments.

Avoid the Premium Trap

Many investors "hunting premium" become elated by the high potential returns available on writes of volatile stocks such as take-over issues, fad stocks, and the like. Time premium for options on these stocks is very high, making them tempting to write. However, economic reasoning providing little basis for initiating writes on extremely volatile stocks. Profit from any dramatic gain in price of the underlying security may be limited to the strike price of the option sold. But participation in all losses past the net proceeds received from selling the option is not limited.

In short, there is no option premium big enough to protect you from a downside break in a volatile situation . . . ask any investor who initiated an option write on a $20 stock because of the "fat" $4 premium that could be earned by selling an option; only to have the stock price drop to the $7 dollar level as the market saw through the phantom fundamentals propping up the stock's price.

Stick to fundamental value, and never write on a stock you wouldn't feel comfortable owning at the net price paid for the optionable stock.

The option page reveals a world of stocks from which to choose. The best way to select them may be through the process of elimination. Don't select those stocks with fundamental characteristics you do not find attractive. From the remainder of the optional stocks, choose a diversified list of fundamentally sound companies that can be analyzed thoroughly and monitored easily. This will enhance familiarity with a company's earnings and a stock's trading patterns, therefore minimizing surprises.

Selling Options Is Prudent Investing

Do you want increased cash flow from your investments? Would you like to reduce the cost of the stocks you buy? Do you want to reduce the risk of owning stocks? Are you puzzled about the right time to sell a stock?

Selling options generates extra earnings from blue-chip securities. This solves the investor's most difficult problem: when is the best time to sell a stock? In effect, that decision is made in advance.

The exercise price of the option helps you establish a target price at which you are willing to sell a stock. The money received by selling the option increases your cash flow. The immediate cash flow has the secondary benefit of reducing the cost of your security and reduces the risk of owning stock.

In a March 1986 article on covered call option writing, *Changing Times* (now called *Kiplinger's Personal Finance*) magazine said: "It's popular among both individual and institutional investors. Many bank trust departments and pension fund managers use it to generate extra income on stocks in their portfolios and as a hedge against price declines." In a bearish, neutral, or bullish market environment, the covered option writer will fare better than the investor who buys and holds only equities.

Option selling has now become so established as a prudent, conservative, low-risk method of investing that it has received official recognition by almost every regulatory body that has control over investments. The Comptroller of the Currency, who regulates the national banks, has ruled that option writing is appropriate for use by bank trust departments in investing their trust funds.

Insurance commissioners of most states have now ruled that insurance companies may use option writing on a portion of their own investments. Various officials entrusted with seeing that pension plans are properly administered have given their blessings to the use of option writing for pension plans. In addition, an enormous number of conservative, professionally managed investment groups have begun using option writing, including church, university, and college endowment funds and union welfare plans. Clearly, the time has now come when the speculative stain should be completely and finally removed from the concept of selling covered options.

"Conservative," means to be more concerned about protecting what one has than with increasing its value through changes in market prices. Option selling protects the investor from declines in the stock price up to the amount of the premium received from the sale of the options. Therefore, using options with stock ownership is more conservative than outright ownership of stock.

Selling options is one of the few forms of investing where one can compute exactly what the return on investment will be if the position is successful. When an investor buys a stock he can compute the dividend, but the results of that investment one year after purchase is going to be determined mostly by what has happened during that time to that stock's price. Here the idea is to continue to own common stock, but to get some downside protection and to take in some profit if the stock stays still or moves up.

Everyone who owns securities should understand and sell options. They can provide investors extra income, set up tax losses, make possible protective hedges, and usually limit losses. But to make money with options, you must work hard, research thoroughly, review often, and follow strict rules.

"Why bother with options at all? In case you haven't noticed, there is risk in stock ownership."
Harvey Friedentag

"Time is what we want most, but what alas! we use worst."
William Penn

CHAPTER *3*

Options and Potential Returns

"Hindsight is always 20:20."
Billy Wilder

If you are unfamiliar with covered call writing, it may seem too complex to be classified as a "simple" strategy, but once you attempt it, you will realize that it is not complex at all.

There are approximately 1,500 optionable stocks, with more pending. With this great number, how can you decide which ones are best for your portfolio?

Let's start with the well known *KISS* strategy—Keep It Simple, Sweetheart—and go on from there.

*Keep it simple.*Don't sell deep-in-the-money options because you hear they are "free money—the stock can't go up that far." This could cause you to sell a good stock for a bad reason.

Keep it safe. Don't exceed your risk tolerance.

Keep it sensible. Just because you read about some alleged mastermind making a killing with options doesn't mean that you should try to copy his operation. Don't try anything that will take you beyond your comfort zone.

Keep it diversified. Gain greater safety through buying different stocks rather than large trades of a single stock.

Finally, and most important!

Keep it disciplined. Losses sometimes occur due to the wrong stock, the wrong strategy, the wrong timing, or just bad luck. More often, losses occur—and get larger—because of a lack of discipline. Whenever you implement an option strategy you should have two points clearly understood in your mind:

1. Set an approximate goal; the point where you expect the strategy to produce profits.
2. Establish an exit point to be used if the trade goes against you.

Don't forget that selling covered call options can be used in their protective capacity as instruments for the transfer and/or reduction of risk. Keep in mind that writing calls against your stock holdings is safer than merely holding the stock. The concept is to continue owning common stock, but to give oneself some downside protection and to take in some profit if the stock stays still or moves up. This approach is not as glamorous as the more risky strategy of buying calls. However, our goal is enhancement and the preservation of capital.

Naked Option Writing

Naked writing is selling an option on something you don't own. When you sell naked options, your major gamble is that the market may move against you. It is very risky and potentially financially ruinous because you must always be ready to buy the stock and then immediately sell it to the option buyer on demand . . . no matter how high the stock has risen in price. Don't sell these uncovered options because they are ballyhooed as a "sure thing." This could produce losses that are fearsome in their magnitude.

Starting a Covered Call Program

If you already own 100 or more shares of an optionable stock, then your decisions are already partly made for you. Since there are always three time frames available, your first question is probably whether you should sell the three-month option, the six-month option, or the nine-month option. The way to decide is to compare the average monthly return for each period. The shortest time frame pays the highest return on a monthly basis. The longer-term options offer a commission savings that should be considered. Also, you may prefer longer-term options to avoid the necessity of multiple transactions for the same period of time.

The Pricing of Options

The most important factors that contribute value to an option contract and influence the premium at which it is traded are the:

- price of the underlying stock (versus strike price); and
- time remaining until expiration (Time Value)

Option Premium = Intrinsic Value + Time Value

Intrinsic Value Explained

If the underlying stock price is in-the-money there is intrinsic value. For example, if an option's strike price is $25 and that stock is trading at $35, the option has intrinsic value of $10.

If the underlying stock price is at-the-money or out-of-the-money there is no intrinsic value.

Time Value Explained

For in-the-money options, the time value premium is the excess portion over the intrinsic value. For at-the-money and out-of-the-money options, the time value premium is the option premium.

These values are in dollars per share. For example, an option contract covering 100 shares of common stock, when trading on the options exchange at "2 points," has a total value of $200 (100 shares × $2 = $200).

Intrinsic Value = Stock Price - Exercise Price

The intrinsic value is always a positive number or zero.

Time Value = Premium Value - Intrinsic Value

The time value of an option premium is the difference between the dollar value of the cash premium and the intrinsic value in dollars of the option contract.

The longer the time remaining until an option's expiration date, the higher the option premium, because there is a greater possibility that the underlying share price might move to make the option in-the-money. The time value of an option does not decrease at a linear rate: it falls off gradually until close to expiration, and then falls off rapidly.

Examples of time and intrinsic values follow.

Example 1 (In-the-Money)
ABC Corp. on May 21 (expiration date)
ABC common stock closed at 35
ABC Corp. August 30 option closed at $8

Intrinsic value	(35 - 30)	=	5
Time value	(8 - 5)	=	3
Total premium			8

Option contracts have a maximum life of nine months. During this period the premium can vary widely, from very low to very high. Their values may be small when the time to expiration is very short, or when there is very little anticipation by option buyers that the market price of the underlying common stock will rise before expiration. Their values will be high when the time to expiration is long, or when the stock is above the strike price.

Example 2 (At-the-Money)
    ABC Corp. on May 21
    ABC common stock closed at 35
    ABC August 35 option closed at 4½

Intrinsic value	=	0
Time value	=	4½
Total premium		4½

August 20th, with ABC valued at $32.50, the option buyer will not call your 100 shares of ABC. You keep the $450 premium money (pre-tax) and write another option on your ABC Corp. stock.

When the *market price* of the common stock is *below or at the strike price* of the option contract, the intrinsic value is zero. In this instance, any value of the premium is entirely time value.

Example 3 (Out-of-the-Money)
    ABC Corp. on May 21
    ABC common stock closed at 35
    ABC Corp. August 40 option closed at $3

Intrinsic Value	= 0
Time value	= 3
Total premium	3

August 20th, with ABC valued at $32.50, the option buyer will not call your 100 shares of ABC. You keep the $300 premium money and write another option on your ABC Corp. stock.

Example 1 (In-the-Money Results)
August 20, with ABC valued at $32.50, the option buyer calls 100 shares of ABC from you at $30.

Sell 100 ABC common at	30
Premium received	8
Total received (per share)	38

August 20th (expiration date) ABC Corp. Stock Price $32.50.

Example 1: In-the-Money . . . . Sell stock, make $300.
Example 2: At-the-Money . . . . Keep $450, do again!
Example 3: Out-of-the-Money . . . . Keep $300, do again!

The stock price when we did the option was at $35.00 per share. We sold 100 shares at $30.00. The option was $800.00.

May 21: 100 ABC at $35.00 . . . . . . $3,500.00 stock value.
August 20: 100 ABC at $32.50 . . . . $3,250.00 stock value.

We have to sell at $30	$3,000.00
plus option money	800.00
Took In (on hand)	3,800.00
Minus (stock value)	3,500.00
Option Net Profit	$300.00

Your net profit is $300. This was the time value of the cash premium of $800 that you received three months previously. Your net profit can never exceed the time value of the option you have sold.

Other factors that give options value and therefore affect the premium are volatility, dividends, and interest rates.

Volatility

Volatility refers to the frequent, large price fluctuations of a stock. This volatility of the underlying share price influences the option premium. The higher the volatility, the higher the premium.

Dividends

The regular cash dividend is paid to the stock owner. Cash dividends affect option premiums through their effect on the underlying share price. Options reflect stock dividends and stock splits because the number of shares represented by each option are adjusted to take these changes into consideration (*e.g.*, one option at $40 becomes two options at $20).

Interest Rates

Higher interest rates tend to result in higher option premiums. That portion of the time value attributable to the interest rate factor will be greater.

Determining the Best Time-Value

In determining how long an option to write, remember that a three-month option will have a higher average monthly return than will a six- or nine-month option.

If your analysis indicates that the stock price will be lower in three-months, it would be to your advantage to write a nine-month contract, which would produce more premium than writing a three-month contract and, on its expiration, writing another three-month contract, and so on.

If your analysis indicates that the stock price will increase in three-months, then it will be to your advantage to write only a three-month contract and on its expiration write another three-month contract, *etc.*, which would total more premium than would an original, nine-month contract. For example:

Stock price on May 21 $50.00	**3-mo***	**6-mo****	**9-mo*****
Aug 50 option premiums	3.00*		
Nov 50 option premiums	3.00*	5.00**	
Feb 50 option premiums	3.00*		6.50***
9-month total premiums	9.00	7.50	6.50

(*Note:* Only half of second six-month premium is included in the total. We sold 2 six-month options in the first 12 months. But are figuring it for just 9 months: one full six-month option and half of second six-month option.)

*sell 3-month option 3 times total premium: $900.

**sell 6-month option 1½ times (one 6-month and half of second 6-month income for 9 months).

***sell one 9-month option for $6.50 income.

If your analysis indicates that in three months the stock may be down 5 and selling at 45, you should sell the long-term option.

Stock price on May 21 $50.00	**3-mo***	**9-mo**
Aug 50 option premiums	3.00	6.50
Nov 50 option premiums	1.00	
Feb 50 option premiums*	1.00	
9-month total premiums*	5.00	6.50

*Stock price drops to $45.00

When the stock price is 45, options with a strike price of 45 probably would have a premium for three months of 2½. You could sell this option after the first option expired, but the risk is that if the price goes up to 50, to buy back the $45 option for $5 would incur a $2.50 loss. Selling the Nov 50 option and getting a 6% return in three months, equaling 24% a year, is hardly losing. We are using averages, and will expect to lose on 10% of the trades.

If you believe that your stock has an expectation of going up during the next three months, then you should sell the shortest-term option. If the stock does as well as you expected, you will be assigned, sell your stock, and be free to reinvest in another optionable security.

If your analysis gives no indication of a stock price rise or fall, you can follow the rule of selling the option that gives you the highest return on a monthly basis.

Determining the Best Strike Price

What are the results of choosing a high strike price rather than a low one? Since your stock has options available at three or more strike prices, which one should you write?

Options with the highest strike price will be the most profitable if the stock goes up, but the option with the lowest strike price will perform the best if the stock goes down.

A lower strike price offers a higher premium. A strike price below the stock price provides a premium including intrinsic value, which gives downside protection. Consider the following example:

When ABC Corp. was selling at 39, its five-month options at that time were priced as follows:

Strike price	Premium
35	5 3/4
40	2 5/8
45	1

When ABC stock remains at 39 until the expiration date of the option, the seller of the 35 option will realize $35 from the exercise of the stock plus the $5.75 premium, a total of $40.75. The seller of the 40 strike price will keep his stock and the premium of 2.62. The seller of the 45 strike price option will keep his stock and will keep the premium of $1.

If the price of the stock had risen to 45, the seller of the 45 option would have done the best. The seller of the 35 option would have $40.75, as above. The seller of the 40 option would receive $40 for his stock plus the $2.62 option premium, a total of $42.62, as before. The seller of the 45 option would have the value of his stock, $45.00, plus the premium of $1, a total of $46. It would appear that the best strategy is to sell the option with the highest strike price.

However, what if the stock had gone *down*? Suppose the price of the stock fell from 39 to 34. None of the options would have been exercised, and each seller would be left with the stock and his premium. Now, each option seller has stock worth $34, and the 35 strike price writer has a premium of $5.75 in his account, the writer of the 40 strike price option has $2.62, and the one who did best in the previous example ends up with just $1.

Which strike price, then, should one write?

To answer this question we must return to the basic reason for selling covered call options. The reason is that the fearless investor is willing to give up a large, *potential*, future gain— which may never happen—in exchange for a certain profit *now*, which is the option premium being paid.

The main reason we are selling covered calls is to obtain an assured income. The one big risk is that the price of the underlying stock will fall. Therefore, my general rule is:

When Selling an Option, Give First Preference to the Option with the Lowest Strike Price

This rule provides the most protection against a decline in the stock's price. If the price of the stock rises, you would have been better off selling at a higher strike price, but you are still making a profit with the lower strike price. When you sell a covered call option, consider that you are giving up possible future "home runs" for a steady stream of "base hits."

"Common sense is the knack of seeing
things as they are, and doing things
as they ought to be done."
Calvin Stowe

In our example, when you sell the 35 strike price option you have made an extra $1.75 on your stock, which is 4.4%. Since this profit will be earned in five months, it means that you are earning an annual rate of 10%. This is great when you consider that the buyer of your option is giving you free insurance for every dollar that your stock could fall down to 35.

If you strongly believe that your stock has a good expectation of rising, you may wish to sell at the highest strike price. You get to keep part of the rise in your stock, and only turn over to the option buyer the excess increase in your stock. Remember, if the price goes down, you will be left with a loss on your stock and only a small premium to cushion that.

Each investor has an opinion of what return on investment is acceptable. This is based on financial conditions and the amount of risk willing to be assumed. Option selling is no different. An option writer accepts a certain amount of risk due to the potential volatility of stock ownership. Therefore, the likely returns from an option sale must exceed those that can be earned on a risk-free investment.

One general guideline, used to set minimum acceptable returns on an option sale, is to seek potential returns of at least double the selected risk-free rate on an if-exercised basis.

Note: Attractive potential returns on high-yield stocks can be found in utilities and some major oil companies. The reason for the attractive return is the stock's dividend. Because these stocks have low volatility, option premiums are small. An option premium would only add marginal income. In such situations, it would be more sensible to buy the stock and own it outright (without selling an option). The option premium provides little in the way of income or downside protection, yet it will limit the upside potential in the stock.

Determining the Best Underlying Stock

If you do not own any optionable stock and would like to sell a covered call option, you have to decide which stock to purchase.

First, you should select a stock that you personally will want to own and hold. For instance, if you decide that there will soon be a downturn in drug stocks' profits and prices, there is no point in buying Merck stock just because it may have a high option premium. Select a stock that you would want to own as if you were not going to be selling options. Remember, if the price of the stock declines, you will still own the stock, and the only risk in selling options (as in owning stock) is that the price of the stock may go down.

Second, you will have to check the quotations to find what the option premiums are for the various stocks. You should select a stock whose option has a high premium. Usually the lower-priced stocks have the higher premiums.

Third, pay attention to the strike prices for the stock you are considering. Remember, the safest option is the one with the lowest strike price. If you are seeking less risk, pick a stock whose option has a strike price below the current market price of the stock. If, after doing all your research, you are optimistic you can pick a stock that has a strike price well above its current price, understanding that this will reduce the amount of your premium and provide little downside protection.

While checking the strike prices available, it is good practice to check not only the current option period, but those for the next three-month period and the one after that, because not all strike prices may be available for future periods. If the price of the stock has declined substantially, then the highest strike price is not going to be offered for the longest time-frame options. If the price of the stock has increased substantially, then the higher strike price may not have opened yet for trading.

Determining When to Take Action

Once you have written an option, you can wait until it expires and then decide which option to write next. In most cases, though, it will be to your advantage to decide whether there are changes that could be made before expiration which will enhance your profit or decrease your downside risk or perhaps both. You will be watching your positions to see if you are earning the maximum amount from the time value of the options you have sold.

Two situations should alert you to action:

1. The current price of any option you have sold declines to a small fraction of its original premium. If any of your outstanding options are selling for 0.25 or less, it is time to act. No matter what happens, the maximum remaining profit you can make from that option is only 25 cents a share and your downside protection is also only 25 cents a share, which is nil. This low price of your outstanding options results from time decay or a decline in the price of your underlying stock.
2. The time value of your outstanding in-the-money options has fallen to a small amount. When this amount begins to approach zero, there is no reason to continue the position. You still have the possibility of loss if the stock declines, but you no longer have the opportunity of a meaningful profit.

Understanding Published Option Premiums

Premiums (prices) for exchange-traded options are published daily in many newspapers. Many investors have some difficulty in understanding the option tables. They are different from the stock tables with which most readers are more familiar.

Thanks are due to *Investor's Business Daily* for introducing an alphabetical option listing and including the volume of contracts. *The Wall Street Journal* finally has started publishing an improved option listing that appears to be the best now available.

A portion of an option table for a trading day is shown in Table 3-1. Though this is only a small part of the total information, it is sufficient for us to obtain an understanding of these listings. It also will allow us to introduce some frequently used words.

To identify the items of information, let's look more closely at the listing for ABC Corp. options. Although we will not be using puts, it is very important to realize where they get listed and never confuse the cash premiums between the types of options.

Table 3-1: *The Wall Street Journal* Format

Option/Strike	Vol	Exch	Last	Net Chg	a-Close	OpenInt
ABC Jun 12½	60	CB	3 1/2	+1/2	16	72
ABC Jun 15	200	CB	1 1/8	+1/4	16	570
ABC Jun 17½ p	40	CB	1 1/2	-1/4	16	660
ABC Jul 15	800	CB	1 1/2	+1/4	16	600
ABC Jul 15 p	80	CB	1/4	-1/8	16	120
ABC Jul 17½	200	CB	1/4	...	16	1000
ABC Aug 15	1300	CB	1 3/4	+3/4	16	408
ABC Aug 15 p	200	CB	1/2	-3/8	16	930
ABC Aug 17½	10	CB	1/2	...	16	812
ABC Aug 20 p	4	CB	4	-1/4	16	25

p-Put

The published table reflects the previous day's trading. Under *Option/Strike* is the name of the underlying security, expiration month, available strike price, and if followed by a *p*, this indicates a put; if blank, a call.

Vol (volume) is the number of trades.

Exc is the exchange on which the option is traded.

Last is the closing price of the option contract.

Net Chg (Net Change) is the difference between the last trading price from one day to the next.

a-Close is the closing price of the underlying security.

OpenInt (Open Interest) is the number of options outstanding.

Table 3-2 shows a format used by a local paper and also reflects the previous day's trading.

In the first column is the name of the underlying security and its closing price.

The second column lists the available strike prices.

The next three columns (Calls-Last) show the closing premium for each of the closing months for which calls are trading.

Table 3-2: Local Paper Format

Options & NY Close	Strike Price	Calls-Last			Puts-Last		
		Jun	July	Aug	Jun	July	Aug
ABC Corp	12 1/2	3 1/2	r*	r	r	r	r
16	15	1 1/8	1 1/2	1 3/4	r	1/4	1/2
16	17 1/2	r	1/4	1/2	1 1/2	r	r
16	20	s**	s	r	s	s	4

*r = no option trades that day.
**s = no such option exists.

The last three columns (Puts-Last) show the closing premium for the each of the closing months in which puts are trading.

In the first example, the in-the-money ABC Corp. August 15 calls closed at 1¾, or $175 per contract.

The out-of-the money ABC Corp. August 17½ calls closed at ½, or $50 per contract.

For purposes of illustration, commissions, transaction costs, and tax considerations are omitted. These factors will definitely affect a strategy's potential outcome, profit or loss, on your income tax return.

Expiration Cycle

A specific optionable stock trades in only one of three cycles. Each cycle is composed of four three-month periods.

The maximum life of an option is about nine months. Expiration dates occur on the third Friday of the month. New nine-month periods commence on the Monday following the third Friday of the month. Options can be traded for the time remaining to their expiration. In addition to the cycles, prior to expiration, trades can be made for a period from one day to the two near-term months plus two additional months of the January, February, or March quarterly cycle (*e.g.*, on the third Friday in January until 4:15 p.m. E.T. a trade covering a period from one day through the end of March is possible). This creates a new, short-term option expiration as seen in Tables 3-3, 3-4, and 3-5 which follow.

Using Option Trading Symbols

When using a computer or terminal for quotes you will need the option trading symbol. This is composed of the stock symbol, the expiration month code, and the strike price code. It is also handy for you to use these when giving orders over

Table 3-3: January Cycle

Expiring Month	*Available Months*			
Jan	Feb	Mar	Apr	Jul
Feb	Mar	Apr	Jul	Oct
Mar	Apr	May	Jul	Oct
Apr	May	Jun	Jul	Oct
May	Jun	Jul	Oct	Jan
Jun	Jul	Aug	Oct	Jan
Jul	Aug	Sep	Oct	Jan
Aug	Sep	Oct	Jan	Apr
Sep	Oct	Nov	Jan	Apr
Oct	Nov	Dec	Jan	Apr
Nov	Dec	Jan	Apr	Jul
Dec	Jan	Feb	Apr	Jul

Table 3-4: February Cycle

Expiring Month	*Available Months*			
Jan	Feb	Mar	May	Aug
Feb	Mar	Apr	May	Aug
Mar	Apr	May	Aug	Nov
Apr	May	Jun	Aug	Nov
May	Jun	Jul	Aug	Nov
Jun	Jul	Aug	Nov	Feb
Jul	Aug	Sep	Nov	Feb
Aug	Sep	Oct	Nov	Feb
Sep	Oct	Nov	Feb	May
Oct	Nov	Dec	Feb	May
Nov	Dec	Jan	Feb	May
Dec	Jan	Feb	May	Aug

Table 3-5: March Cycle

Expiring Month		Available Months		
Jan	Feb	Mar	Jun	Sep
Feb	Mar	Apr	Jun	Sep
Mar	Apr	May	Jun	Sep
Apr	May	Jun	Sep	Dec
May	Jun	Jul	Sep	Dec
Jun	Jul	Aug	Sep	Dec
Jul	Aug	Sep	Dec	Mar
Aug	Sep	Oct	Dec	Mar
Sep	Oct	Nov	Dec	Mar
Oct	Nov	Dec	Mar	Jun
Nov	Dec	Jan	Mar	Jun
Dec	Jan	Feb	Mar	Jun

the telephone to your broker. With use these will become second nature to you.

The expiration month and strike price codes are listed in Table 3-6.

The ticker/quotation symbol for the stock is used first, followed by the month and the strike price codes. For example, ABCLW is ABC Dec 17 1/2 call. ABCFF is ABC Jun 30. XYZHX is XYZ Aug 22 1/2.

Examples of last three columns of the price codes: CCIGG, Citicorp, July 35; DDAK, Dupont, Jan. 55; AMEEE, Ametek, May 25; TJL, AT&T, Oct. 60.

The option expiration months are the two near-term months plus the two additional months in the January, February, or March quarterly cycle.

For listed stock options, the expiration date is the Saturday following the third Friday of the expiration month. That is the deadline by which brokerage firms must submit exercise notices to the OCC. The exchanges and brokerage

Table 3-6 Expiration Month and Strike Price

Month	Codes		Call	Strike Price Codes		
January	A	A	5	105	205	305
February	B	B	10	110	210	310
March	C	C	15	115	215	315
April	D	D	20	120	220	320
May	E	E	25	125	225	325
June	F	F	30	130	230	330
July	G	G	35	135	235	335
August	H	H	40	140	240	340
September	I	I	45	145	245	345
October	J	J	50	150	250	350
November	K	K	55	155	255	355
December	L	L	60	160	260	360
		M	65	165	265	365
		N	70	170	270	370
		O	75	175	275	375
		P	80	180	280	380
		Q	85	185	285	385
		R	90	190	290	390
		S	95	195	295	395
		T	100	200	300	400
		U	7 1/2			
		V	12 1/2			
		W	17 1/2			
		X	22 1/2			

firms have rules and procedures regarding deadlines for an option holder to notify his brokerage firm of his intention to exercise. Contact your broker for specific deadlines.

The Standard Method of Using Options

If assigned, the profit or loss is the sum of the premium plus the difference, if any, between the strike price and the original stock price. If the stock price rises above the strike price, the stock will be called away and the opportunity to profit from further increases in the stock price is lost. If the stock price declines, hedging protects against loss to the extent of the premium.

When the underlying stock stays the same, you win when selling out-of-the-money options or at-the-money options. You keep the premium and your stock.

When the underlying stock goes up in value so does the option premium. In the standard manner of option selling your stock would be assigned.

My Method of Using Options

All the "experts" in the stock market field will say, "The writer of an option, in return for the cash premium received, forgoes the opportunity to benefit from an increase in the stock price that exceeds the strike price of the option. The option writer continues to bear the risk of a sharp decline in the price of the stock. The cash premium received will only slightly offset this loss." *This is not correct!*

Using Fungibility

An option writer may cancel the obligation anytime before being assigned by executing a closing purchase transaction, buying back the option that was previously sold—a fungible action. The writer of an option, in return for the premium received, uses the opportunity to benefit from an increase in the stock price.

Stock Price Is No Longer a Concern

With my method you no longer care about the price of the stock that you bought. Investors normally watch their stock's price go up and down and sideways. With my method, when the stock does go down we would buy back the option at a very inexpensive price and immediately write it again. Perhaps we took in a premium of 2 and could close it out by buying the option for 25 cents. If the stock price went down $5 we would write a new option at a strike price $5 lower. Since you already lost when the stock declined, using my method you are always taking in additional premium income, which will help offset the decline in the stock price.

When the stock does not reach the strike price, let the option expire, keep the premium income, and write a new option at the same strike price.

When the stock goes up, you could let the option go at a profit (as in the standard method). With my method, you would buy the option back and immediately write a new option at a higher strike price, reflecting the gain in the stock price. The second premium added to the first will help defray the cost.

During the months of existence of most option contracts, the option price and also the stock price will vary and fluctuate. The time value portion of the option always represents a judgment determined by the traders. Changes in the time value or the intrinsic value occur continuously during the market trading hours, either of which affect the option price.

For the buyer, the option contract is a wasting asset to own; its value decays as time passes. The time value portion of the option premium value always is zero at expiration. Selling the time value repeatedly, for the same underlying stock, makes options work for you.

By using these principles and the ones discussed in the next chapters, you will learn to react to the stock market.

You will not be looking for the stock to go up to make money. You will be making money on the wasting asset called time value. Your plan is to get gains from the time values of options you have sold. Your philosophy about the stock market will be changed. You will be counting real cash premiums put into your account by the speculators.

> *"Once you are moving in the direction*
> *of your goals . . . nothing can stop you."*
> Anonymous

> *"On the plus side, death is one of the few things*
> *that can be done as easily lying down . . ."*
> Woody Allen

CHAPTER *4*

Margin–The Credit You Can Use

"A bank is a place where they lend you an umbrella in fair weather and ask for it back when it begins to rain."
Robert Frost

I have been using margin in my option income portfolio since the Crash of 1987. That was the opportunity for which I had been waiting: to buy common stocks at up to a 50% discount. The money to pay for the purchases came from my use of margin. Margin is the borrowing of money against the market value of a portfolio. The use of margin enabled me to buy more stocks. It is one investment tool I choose to use.

As an investor, you are in business—the business of investing in other businesses through the ownership of common stock. Those shares are your inventory. When you add to your inventory at bargain prices, you will have more shares to sell options against, thus enhancing your earnings. It is good practice to purchase a widely diversified portfolio of strong company stocks, and by borrowing against your stock portfolio, to buy more shares. Again, this enables you to sell more options, thus increasing your profits. Through diversification you are spreading your risk among many companies whose stocks may advance or decline at different times. The average of rises and declines, over a long period, tends to even out.

Today I owe more in my margin account than I ever have owed in my entire life. Nevertheless, I still believe in fiscal responsibility, and I have no other debt.

Your stocks can act as security when borrowing money for any purpose through your margin account. Using your margin for purposes other than your investment portfolio could be hazardous to your wealth by jeopardizing your investment plan.

The simple fact is that the use of credit in buying and selling stocks can be no worse or no better than the use of credit in any other business. The skill and judgment of the user of the credit are what is important.

> *"Credit is like a looking-glass, which, when once sullied by a breath, may be wiped clear again; but if once cracked can never be repaired."*
> Walter Scott

Our great American economy is built, based, and continues to grow on borrowed money. The federal, state, and local governments borrow and service huge amounts of debt. That debt is incurred to attend to the present and future needs of the citizens. Such borrowing is done with Treasury bills, notes, bonds, and municipal bonds.

Every large corporation has debt for future growth, expansion, and research and development. Business people borrow to start and fund their companies using credit or loans to finance their operations.

Most of us buy our homes, cars, and other large purchases using personal credit rather than waiting until we can pay cash. The people who provide and make the things we want have the benefit of employment. They in turn can go out and use credit to get the things that they want or need. Our credit-based economy brings us the high standard of living we enjoy.

With many, margin (credit) has a bad reputation. "What? Borrow to gamble on the stock market?" "Remember all those people who jumped from rooftops in 1929 because of margin!" "Every time a stock bought on margin drops in price, you have to put up more cash." Such statements represent an uninformed viewpoint.

Advantages of Margin

To use margin, you should understand it thoroughly. The use of margin generally incurs greater risk and portfolio volatility. Yet, greater rewards are possible with the prudently planned use of margin. Over a long time period, as the market goes up and margin is effectively employed, margin buying gives the portfolio leverage. In financial terms leverage means using your money and borrowed money to increase the total rate of return.

The fact is you will have more shares, with the safety of wider stock diversification. This provides increased total return, and more safety than cash alone would permit you to buy. During market declines, although your losses are leveraged, they are manageable and of a shorter duration than market rises, if you don't sell.

The margin loan is open-ended. It has no specific time limits. No specific installments are due nor principal payments required. The cost of borrowing on margin is very low. Margin loan interest rates are comparable to, if not lower than, the prime interest rate offered to a bank's best business customers. Within certain limits, margin loan interest can be tax-deductible, as well.

Applying to use margin is fast and easy. It is part of the application for a brokerage account. There is no credit screening since your stocks in the account provide collateral.

In theory, the margin debt is callable. You should carefully read the margin agreement papers you must sign. I have never heard of a margin debt called other than to meet the minimum legal requirement.

The cost of borrowing on margin is based on the "Broker's Call Rate," a figure published daily in the financial press, plus a percentage added by your broker. For example, the broker's call rate can be found under "Money Rates" listed as "Call Money." A brokerage representative can tell you the current margin rates.

Margin Interest

Margin interest is based on the total amount of the margin loan. Avoid having more than one margin account; it will save you interest because the larger the loan the lower the interest rate. If you have multiple margin accounts, you can transfer into one account without having to sell anything. This makes consolidating margin accounts easy.

Margin interest is calculated with the following percentages added to the broker's call rate. For example:

Amount of Loan ($)	Broker Add-On (%)
0-9,999	2.00
10,000-24,999	1.50
25,000-49,999	1.00
50,000+	0.50

Table 4-1 compares margin rates with other interest rates.

Your brokerage statement will report your current margin-buying power (the amount of securities you can pur-

---

Table 4-1: Margin Rates versus Other Interest Rates (January 1994)

Broker Call Loan Rate	5.00%
$10,000 Margin Loan	6.50%
Prime Rate	6.00%
Credit Card Rate	18.00%

---

chase with available marginable securities), your outstanding margin debt, the interest incurred for the period,
and the interest rate for the period. You can get an up-to-
the-minute report by calling your broker.

Interest charges only begin upon settlement. Once you
decide to use margin, the interest rate based on the broker's call rate will be charged and posted to your account
each day until you pay off the loan, or until you sell the
securities used as collateral.

Payback on the loan is at your convenience and there
is no fixed payment schedule. Any dividends or interest
from the securities used as collateral may be applied to
reducing the balance.

A benefit of using margin is that it allows you to use
the value of your assets without selling them. You don't
have to consider liquidating stocks that are doing well
when another attractive investment opportunity comes
along. You don't have to realize a profit and pay tax on the
sale of stock to use the money.

Opening a Margin Account

There is no charge for opening a margin account. Margin
is an additional feature of a brokerage account. If you have
one, adding margin requires only that you:

- read, understand, complete, sign, and return a
  margin agreement;
- once approved, purchase or deposit eligible securities in your account to be used as collateral;
- instruct your brokerage representative to deposit
  your securities in a type 2 margin account (type 1 is
  a cash account); and
- ask your brokerage representative for the amount of
  cash available or additional buying power you
  have.

Important Margin Principles

Borrow Less than the Full Loan Value

By borrowing less than the full loan value of your securities, you can still employ leverage and low-cost borrowing. You reduce the chance of having dramatic market fluctuations place you in a "margin call" (maintenance) situation.

Borrow Against Conservative Investments

Borrow only against sound stocks, those with proven track records and dividend payment histories. The risk of margin call situations can be lessened considerably.

Borrow Against a Diversified Portfolio

It would be highly unlikely that all stocks would go down substantially and simultaneously. Some stocks would go lower, some stocks would go higher, and many would retain the same values.

Margin Terminology

Equity is securities value due debit balance. For example, equity would be $30,000 in a margin account with stocks worth $40,000 and a debit balance of $10,000.

Market Value is the price at which a security is currently trading.

Mark-to-the Market is the revaluing of a margin account to assure compliance with maintenance requirements. Daily gains and losses are reflected by this process.

Debit Balance is money a margin customer owes a broker.

Credit Balance is money a broker owes a customer.

How do these terms work together? Here is the equation:

Market Value - Debit Balance = Equity

Market price fluctuations increase or decrease market value and equity.

Margin interest increases debit balance, and decreases equity.

Expired options and dividends increase equity and decrease the debit balance.

Portfolio Valuation

Having opened a margin account with $7,500 cash or marginable securities, if $2,500 is borrowed to buy more stock, the portfolio would consist of $10,000 worth of stock, a $2,500 debit balance, and equity value of $7,500, as shown in the following portfolio financials:

Marginable Stocks Market Value	$10,000
Debits (loans, margin interest)	-2,500
Equity (net worth)	$7,500

Market Value - Debit Balance = 75% Account Equity

The annual dividends will more than cover the annual margin costs:

Marginable Stocks Market Value	$10,000
Dividend Income ($10,000 @ 3.5%)	350 annual
Margin Interest ($2,500 @ 7.0 %)*	-175 annual

*Broker's call loan rate 5% + 2% broker add-on.

The seasoned margin user spends appreciated gains to buy more stock to bring the portfolio to a 25% margined level. This presents no more risk than the original decision to use margin.

The decline in the price of one stock will not by itself create a margin call, since evaluation of a margin account is based on the entire portfolio.

Securities valued at less than $5.00 per share have no loan value. Certain over-the-counter stocks are also not marginable. Call your brokerage representative for details.

Margin Call

The *margin call* is literally a call from your broker asking you to add assets to your margin account. The Federal Reserve policy governing margin requires a call when the amount owed is more than 25% of the current value of your margin account. Brokerage firms may set their own, higher margin levels.

Your equity (market value - debit balance = % equity) must drop to 30% before there will be a margin call. Generally, you are given five business days to meet a margin call. With some brokers, the margin call is met if the market value of your portfolio increases in price by the fifth day.

Portfolio value	$10,000
Debit balance	-7,500
Equity 25%	2,500
Margin call add to account	500
Equity 30%	$3,000

A margin call can be met with cash or additional stock deposits into the account.

Since we are investing without fear, we do not anticipate ever receiving a margin call.

> *"We cannot direct the wind,*
> *but we can adjust the sails."*
> Anonymous

Converting Dividends into Capital Gains

Margin interest is deductible against dividend income. Generally, the dividend yields gained from a total portfolio will tend to offset the margin interest. As the use of margin provides the opportunity of owning a larger stock portfolio, greater capital gains result. Upon selling the stock the growth in value is taxed at the favorable long-term capital gains rate, whereas the dividends would have been taxed as ordinary income.

In the next chapter I'll show you how you can manage an option income portfolio.

> *"Money and time are the heaviest burdens of life, and the unhappiest of all mortals are those who have more of either than they know how to use."*
> Samuel Johnson

CHAPTER **5**

Managing an
Option Income Portfolio

*"Half of our life is spent trying to find
something to do with the time we have rushed
through life trying to save."*
Will Rogers

Goals and Objectives

The option income portfolio approach in selling covered
call options endeavors to:

- minimize risk;
- provide diversification;
- maximize capital gains potential, dividend income,
  options premium income, and downside protection;
- create portfolios of options with the objective of
  earning attractive, consistent returns on investment
  throughout the stock market cycle; and
- increase long-term capital appreciation and income
  from stock ownership.

The option income portfolio is a continuous investment
strategy. Stock should be owned and options sold. Dividends and option premiums can be earned and capital
gains increased. Thus, another step toward investing
without fear.

Selling options with the strike price near the current
market price of the stock usually results in a most balanced

combination of potential returns and downside protection. The potential will exist for stock appreciation. Meanwhile, a substantial amount of option premium will be earned that will provide downside protection.

Investors generally have two objections to option selling. They may lose if a stock's price declines past the break-even point. They may limit the upside potential if a stock's price appreciates more than the premium.

Limiting an account to one or two option positions increases the odds that one of these unfavorable events will occur. By creating a diversified portfolio among several stocks and their options, losses on one position may be offset by gains on another.

Assuming the portfolio of stocks selected performs about equally to the stock market, continuous option selling as described above should do better than the market. In addition, total returns will be greater over time.

The asset base for an option income portfolio should consist only of common stocks for which option contracts are routinely traded on option exchanges.

There are many stocks from which you regularly might generate 25% per year (gross) using options. This gross income can be captured by the conservative investor. The buyer of the options will pay a cash premium for the right to buy stock at the strike price until expiration of the option contract.

The option contract, a wasting asset, decays in value as time passes. It is only the time value component of the option contract— not the intrinsic value—that wastes as the time of expiration grows near. At expiration the time value is zero.

Time value becomes a source of profit as a new option is sold on the same underlying stock. Because the time value sale can be repeated continuously and indefinitely, the profit from time value is a certainty. As one contract expires, a new contract is sold on the same round lot of stock.

Though an option income portfolio can be operated with as few as one to five different stocks, for safety it is advisable to increase the number of companies represented in a portfolio. The number of stocks owned would probably not exceed 20. It is at this level that diversity and reasonable safety is achieved. As with all businesses, when initial capital is lower than it ought to be, you make compromises. You must accept some higher cost and risk. Chapter 6 will deal with the problem of insufficient capital.

There are rarely more than 20 optionable stocks that will have options selling with acceptable time values in their option premiums. Most time values are too low. Always be on the lookout for higher time values.

As opinions become more favorable on the outlook for a specific stock, the time value in the option premium becomes larger. Sell stocks that no longer have large enough time value premiums compared to the ones you could replace them with, and buy stocks that have larger time values. Follow these changing time values in the financial press.

The Writing Possibilities

As a review, recall that the strike price comes in three choices:

1. *At-the-money:* The strike price and the stock price are the same. The buyer pays for time value only, as there is no intrinsic value.
2. *In-the-money:* The strike price is below the stock price. The buyer pays for intrinsic and time value.
3. *Out-of-the-money:* The strike price is above the stock price. The buyer pays less for time value, and there is no intrinsic value.

With a little practice you can quickly scan the option page and identify the good writes. Look at the three-month option column. Look for premiums where the time value is

5%-10% of the stock price. Underline each and go on. In a short time you will have 5 to 10 candidates. Now use the stock and option selection formula:

Time Value ÷ Today's Stock Price = Percentage

Percentage × Sales per Year = Annualized Percentage

The annualized percentage will serve as a realistic guide to the most profitable writes. At this time you may wish to do your fundamental buy-and-hold analysis on each selected stock. Choose the finalist for your option income portfolio.

Stocks and their options tend to rise and fall over the weeks and months. At times there may be no stock candidates to study. At other times there will be more candidates than you can possibly buy. There is never a rush in this business; if you miss one today, there will be ample time to find another. This permits you the time to research your candidates. Everything constantly changes. The stock market is a living, breathing enterprise. Yesterday's closing prices will be different when you call your broker the next morning. *Remember: don't chase stocks and their options!*

Stock Selection for Option Writing

You will have a different mindset than the average stock investor, who is looking for a stock that will go up in price. Your planned gains arise from the time values of the options you will sell. This is an unusual approach to stock selection. Most investors select stocks on either fundamental analysis or technical analysis. You will use the time values of a stock, tempered by fundamental analysis and the long-term hold principles as discussed.

To select a stock for your option income portfolio, you must have available a current option page from which to select a stock that has the most profitable time value in its option premiums. If this stock meets your criteria, buy it as an underlying stock.

To get an annual return of 20 to 40% you must find available option premiums whose time value will produce a return of 5 to 10% in three months on the price of the stock. Using the option page, mentally calculate the percentage of the stock purchase price that the time value represents. Of the more than 1,500 optionable stocks, in all probability, you will only have some five to ten stocks to consider. If the time value seems attractive, then turn to fundamental analysis to make your decision.

Approximately 20 investment strategies use stocks and options; you will be using only one, writing option contracts. At expiration, you will sell a new option contract on the next 90-day maturity. This investment strategy attempts to achieve the maximum gross profit while keeping expenses down, thus generating as great a net profit as possible. The main expenses will be stockbrokerage commissions.

Stockbrokerage Commissions

Commissions for option trading are less than those for the purchase and sale of common stocks. Keep stock turnover at a minimum. Sell stocks only when there is a real reason (*e.g.*, the time value of the premium is smaller than that available from another stock).

Commission expense with options, as with stocks, is less per trade when you are dealing with more volume or value. There are savings on commissions when you buy multiple contracts on options. Five contracts don't cost much more than one. There is an economy in size to consider when trading options.

Buy/Write Strategy

Make a time value comparison of optionable stocks you own. If a stock rates poorly, sell it and buy a promising one. Otherwise, immediately sell an option to protect yourself against a price decline and to generate current income.

On buying an optionable stock, you should protect yourself immediately against a price decline. *Buy/write* is the investment strategy of purchasing stock and writing options simultaneously. This conservative approach generates maximum current income by use of option premiums. A buy/write should be considered a buy/*right* as it is the best way to buy new stock for the option income portfolio.

Example: Tell your broker to buy 200 shares of ABC common stock and write to open two contracts of the ABC September 10 call options with a net debit to you of $9.00.

By doing a buy/write order, if the stock price was $10 and the three-month call was $1, the amount owed would be the difference of $9 per share or $1,800 plus commissions.

Right here is where the back cover is true: "You will receive many times the price of this book on your first transaction." By using a buy/write an investor is always ahead on day one.

When buying a stock and selling an option, a cash premium is received that has two components—intrinsic value and time value. The strike price is the agreed upon selling price of the stock for 90 days.

Option Premium = Intrinsic Value + Time Value

Buy ABC for $10.00 a share	- $10.00
Sell an ABC 10 option for 90 days	+ 1.00
Out of pocket	- $9.00
Total agreed price and premium	$11.00

You made 10% in 90 days (40% annualized). You can figure the desirability of stock/option choices from time values alone, as derived from the option premium, stock cost, and strike price. You do not need to add the dividends, stockbrokerage commissions, and margin interest, as this often complicates a simple procedure. Remember, we are selling time—when an option contract expires, the contract is void forever. The option maturity months are integral to the quotations. A typical quotation for a specific option appears below. At a strike price of $20, this option is in-the-money by 7/8 ($0.875).

Date: April 21 (April options have expired)

	Jul	*Oct*	*Jan*	*NY Close*
ABC Corp. 20	2 7/8	4 3/8	5 1/2	20 7/8

Intrinsic value is $0.875, time value for July is $2, for Oct $3.50, and Jan is $4.625. The stock closed that day at $20.875. If you sold one ABC Corp. July 20 option contract at $2.875 per share for the 100-share contract, you would receive $287.50 gross income. You would receive $437.50 for October and $550.00 for the January option contract.

It is advantageous to do three-month timeframes on option contracts, instead of six-month and nine-month contracts. The premium money looks larger at first for doing a nine month contract but note the results below, if the time value remained the same.

Three-Month Contract Nine-Month Contract

First contract	$287.50	$550.00
Second contract	287.50	
Third contract	287.50	
Gross	$862.50	Gross $550.00

You will realize $312.50 more ($862.50 - $550.00 = $312.50) by writing consecutive three-month contracts. Other advantages will be discussed later.

On buying a new stock and selling a short-term call, if you are mid-cycle for the 90-day contract, do not sell a call for the next expiration date, but go to the second expiration.

Formula for Stock and Option Selection

If an option is written at-the-money or out-of-the money the option premium is all time value. The in-the-money option will have time value plus the intrinsic value above the strike price.

The formula for computing estimated "annualized" rates of return in percent is:

$$\text{Time Value} \div \text{Today's Stock Price} = \text{Percentage}$$

$$\text{Percentage} \times \text{Sales per Year*} = \text{Annualized Percentage}$$

*For example, using 3-month option periods,
we could effect four sales per year.

Using the April 21 example above, for the July, October, and January options the percentages are as follows:

July
$20.00 $2.00 \div 20.875 = 9.6\% \times 4 = 38\%$

October
$20.00 $3.50 \div 20.875 = 16.8\% \times 2 = 33\%$

January
$20.00 $4.625 \div 20.875 = 22.2\% \times 1.25 = 27\%$

Four three-month options can be sold during a year, two six-month options, and one and a quarter nine-month options.

Using this formula will permit you to do your percentage calculations rapidly.

Within the last two or three days of an expiring option, if the stock price is below the strike price or even with it, the option will expire worthlessly. If your stock price is above the strike price (in-the-money) at expiration, you can either let them have it (normal method), or you can buy the fungible option back before expiration, keep the stock, and write it again at a higher strike price. After the expiration in July, assuming we wrote the option in April, we would look at the October expiration, the next one available on the three-month cycle after July. You must learn to react prior to the option expiration.

The whole essence of operating an option income portfolio is investing without fear. We have a method that guarantees a steady income by selling time only and does not try to make profits in the irrational market. We are no longer stock pickers. We are not trying to capture those elusive stock price swings by being market timers. We are just cashing-in on the decaying time values that we are selling.

The Option Buyer

After many years of selling options, I still marvel that such an opportunity exists when I see the option monies come in. I have the option buyers to thank for making this possible. There are more option buyers than there are option sellers, which helps keep the option premiums up.

You must understand that the option buyers are speculating. They plan for the stock price to rise sharply beyond the premium value which they paid to you and that the option contract can be sold at a profit before expiration without buying or calling the underlying stock.

The contract that you sold once may be traded dozens of times. You will not care about this fact. The buyers are gambling with small amounts of money, and do not have the cash to buy your stock from you. They do not want the stock. They want the rapid, leveraged gains that can occasionally be made.

An Option Income Portfolio Is a Proven Winner

With options we have a win-win-win situation; with only stocks a win-lose-draw.

Underlying Stock Price	*Declines*	*Increases*	*Same*
Stock with Options	Win	Win	Win
Stock Only	Lose	Win	Same

If the stock price increases, you keep the time value portion of the premium received, even if the option-holder exercises the right to buy your stock. The intrinsic portion of the option goes to the buyer of the option. Though it may appear that you give up the gain in a large price rise which you would have had if you had not sold an option, you will use it to your advantage. In a small price rise, if the cash premium received is larger than the rise in the stock price, your gain will be larger than the gain in the stock price.

If the stock price stays the same, the option expires and you keep the option premium received.

In a price decline, if the option premium received is larger than the decline, you have no loss and possibly still have a gain. The only risk is when the stock price goes lower than the cost of your underlying stock and the cash premium received. It is precisely at this time that you should buy back the option for pennies on the dollar and immediately write a new option. You will always be taking in money, and this income will act like a parachute in a stock price decline.

This will protect you. You have reduced the possibility of a loss, but not eliminated it. The stock market is irrational, and any stock price has an equal probability of going up or down. Using the guidelines of this book, you can react to the market and use the basic stock market principles for investing without fear.

You have just learned how to protect your option income portfolio from a decline in stock market price value while you sell covered call options.

Option Follow-Up Action

Once an option is sold it must be monitored, since follow-up action must be taken at or before the expiration of the option . . . even if it is just a decision to allow it to expire.

Some investors prefer a passive approach. They allow the stock to be called if its price is above the strike price at expiration. They rewrite an option if the stock price is below the strike price at expiration. This approach is simple and functional, but more active management creates greater profits.

Follow-up action on an option is guided by movements in the underlying stock's price and by the passage of time. Consideration is also given to the stock price in relation to the strike price of the option sold.

Option selling is a strategy designed to provide a balance of returns consisting of potential for stock appreciation, income, and downside protection. As time passes or the underlying stock fluctuates in price, this balance will change. Once the balance changes, it is time to consider action to restore the position to its original balance, or liquidate it.

"The man on top of the mountain didn't fall there."
Anonymous

Periodical Review of Portfolio Equity Holdings

Buy more Stock? Sell the Stock? Hold the Stock? Informed investors agree that periodical reviews of their portfolio equity holdings are part of the investment process. In its most simple form, the investor looks at each equity holding and asks whether it should still be held. Are the fundamental and other reasons for which this stock was purchased still in effect? Should it be sold? Has the stock met a set objective or changed to the point where holding it can no longer be justified?

A more elaborate review process would add a third question. Should we be adding to our current holdings because the stock has moved down to an attractive buying range? This simple review process can be summarized by questioning whether a holding should be bought (adding to positions), held (doing nothing), or sold (liquidating).

Some investors might answer as follows:

1. Would I add to this position? Yes, but at a lower price.
2. Would I sell this stock? Yes, at the current price.
3. Would I sell this stock? Yes, but at a higher price.

Let us refine our review process and ask our questions as follows:

1. Would I be willing to add to this position if my costs were 10% below the current market price?
2. Would I be willing to liquidate my stock at a price 10% above the current market price?

Investors who answer yes to both questions can either wait for the stock to move up or down 10% before taking action. Or they can use options, take immediate action, and create an opportunity to increase the return of their holdings, even if the selling or buying target is not realized.

Here is how it works. Investors who are willing to sell a holding at a higher price can write call options against their holdings. At expiration, if the stock price exceeds the strike price the stock is sold.

Investors who add new stock could write calls at the stock price or lower. The premium received could be thought of as a discount on the stock.

For investors who are willing to sell their holdings at a higher price and add to their positions at a lower price, this is a key strategy to consider. Table 5-1 shows a hypothetical portfolio and options. For simplification taxes and commissions have not been factored in.

Now assume the holders of the portfolio in the table are willing to sell any of the holdings 10% above the current market price. They would also be willing to double-up at a cost of 10% below the current market price.

With ABC stock at $43 1/4, this implies an effective selling price of $47 5/8 and a purchase price of $38 7/8 is required to meet these objectives.

Should the investor sell the stock at $45, he will get to keep the premium. Thus the effective selling price will be $47 5/8, which was the target.

If the price of ABC fell to $41 5/8 the investor could buy more at that price, and with the premium received reach the target of $38 7/8.

TABLE 5-1: (October Calendar Date— January Option Quotes)

Stock Symbol	Stock Price	Series	Price
ABC	43 1/4	Jan 45	2 5/8
LMN	90 1/2	Jan 95	2 13/16
XYZ	23 1/4	Jan 25	1

As you can see in Table 5-2, the 10% above, 10% below objectives can easily be met. With covered call options, investors can increase the return of their holdings when neither the buying or selling targets are met. Looking again at ABC stock, if at the January expiration the stock is trading at the same price, it is highly unlikely that the option will be assigned. It will expire worthlessly. In this case the investor keeps the $2 5/8 per share and repeats the operation selling the April 45 calls.

Table 5-2: (January Expiration—Required Prices To Reach Target)

Stock Symbol	Stock Price	Sell Price	Buy Price
ABC	43 1/4	47 5/8	40 5/8
LMN	90 1/2	97 13/16	87 5/8
XYZ	23 1/4	26	22 1/4

The returns for our stock portfolio in a flat market can be seen in Table 5-3. They would be enhanced further by any dividends received on the stocks held.

Table 5-3: (January Expiration—Annualized Returns in a Flat Market)

Stock Symbol	Stock Price	Total Premium	Total %	Annualized %
ABC	43 1/4	2 5/8	6.0%	24.0%
LMN	90 1/2	2 13/16	3.2%	12.8%
XYZ	23 1/4	1	3.3%	13.2%

As illustrated, the mechanics of covered calls are quite simple, and the strategy offers excellent returns in flat and rising markets, while letting the investor average down in falling markets. The following points should be taken into account before establishing a position.

1. Ten percent up/down targets. There is no magic to the 10% targets selected in these examples. These are realistic expectations for stocks with average volatility. Wider targets can be established for more volatile stocks (whose option premiums are normally higher). Narrower targets should be considered for lower volatility stocks. Targets may be established for longer or shorter option periods.

2. Time horizon. A three- to five-month time will let investors set targets that meet their realistic expectations. This may provide an adequate return in flat markets. When they establish the strategy; investors must ask themselves: "Would I be willing to sell/buy my stock 10% above/below the current market price during the next three to five months?"

3. Future stock value. In our examples, when selling a call, the strike prices were close to the current stock price. You will probably sell a call at a higher strike price if you are bullish on the stock and sell at a lower strike price if you are bearish on the stock.

4. New positions. Covered calls need not be limited to stocks already in the portfolio. An investor can use a buy/write to simultaneously purchase a stock and sell covered calls against these shares.

Follow-up action mainly consists of monitoring the prices of the stock and the option, taking no action if the underlying stock and its option price go up or remain the same until option expiration week. It is at this time that the decision is made to either do nothing and have your stock assigned or buy the option back, keeping your stock (closing out the option). If the underlying stock and its option price go down, wait until expiration and let it expire worthless. A better strategy is to buy it back early in the option period, cancel the contract, and rewrite a new, lower strike price option for the next expiration cycle.

How can we determine when to buy back? The following questions must be considered:

1. Is the time premium remaining on the option less than one quarter of the time premium received? If so, it is time to consider writing a new option, as most of the profit from this position has been made.
2. Is the price of the option less than one quarter of the premium received? If so, it is time to consider writing a new option as minimal downside protection remains.
3. Is the stock about to go ex-dividend? If so it may be necessary to buy back the option to protect the receipt of the dividend.

An affirmative answer to any of these questions should trigger a review of the position and consideration of follow-up action.

Option Income Portfolio Summary

Do not wish (or pray) for a profitable trade. Always make trading decisions based on sound analysis.

Ideally, you should own several common stocks in different industries. Diversify, diversify, diversify! This cannot be stressed enough!

Do not let others influence your trading decisions. Stick to your guns.

Attempt to select stocks having options expiring in different months.

Use limit orders in your operation.

Let dividend income pay the margin interest costs and option premiums reduce the margin debit balance. Then borrow more on margin to buy more stocks and write more options.

Do not trade just to trade. Many people enjoy trading for the excitement of the action. Maintain your present position when there are no definite trading opportunities. Be patient and disciplined; opportunities will appear.

> *"A scissors grinder is the only person whose business is good when things are dull."*
> Anonymous

> *"If thou wouldst keep money, save money;*
> *If thou wouldst reap money, sow money."*
> Thomas Fuller

CHAPTER 6

Option Income Portfolio as a Tax Shelter

"In 1790, the nation which had fought a revolution against taxation without representation discovered that some of its citizens were not much happier about taxation with representation."
Lyndon B. Johnson

What you have left after taxes is your real income. By employing the techniques described in this book, you can reduce, defer, or eliminate taxes on investment income. Investments that produce only income are not only exposed to inflation, but are also fully exposed to taxation. Protect yourself from the tax consequences of your success. If you have even modest income or profits, you will be forced to consider tax planning and tax sheltering. Tax factors will effect your buy and sell decisions in operating your option income portfolio.

Investment Taxation Definitions

To avoid confusion, several widely accepted investment definitions are presented below.

Capital Asset is a long-term asset that is not bought or sold in the normal course of business. The IRS considers both stocks and options to be capital assets.

Capital Gain is the amount by which the proceeds from the sale of a capital asset exceed the cost of acquiring it.

Capital Loss is the amount by which the proceeds from the sale of a capital asset are less than the cost of acquiring it.

Capital Loss Carry-Forward is the capital loss which exceeds capital gains and the allowed annual limit of $3,000 against ordinary income. It may be carried forward to subsequent years as an offset to capital gains or ordinary income. There is no limit to the amount of capital losses that may be used to offset capital gains in any one year. Only losses exceeding gains may be used to offset ordinary income.

Cost Basis is the original price of a stock, including stock-brokerage commissions.

Earned Income is income from wages, salaries, bonuses, and commissions generated by providing goods or services.

Fungible means something of identical quality and is interchangeable. (Commodities such as soybeans or wheat, common shares of the same company, and dollar bills are all familiar examples.) A fungible unit is any unit that can replace another unit, as in discharging a debt or obligation.

Fungibility is the interchangeability of listed options, by virtue of their common expiration dates and strike prices. Fungibility makes it possible for buyers and sellers to close out their positions by using offsetting transactions through the Options Clearing Corporation.

Long-Term and *Short-Term* for taxes is the holding period required to differentiate short-term gain or loss from long-term gain or loss for tax purposes.

Offset (accounting) is the amount equaling or counter-balancing another amount on the opposite side of the ledger. Capital gains can be offset by capital losses.

Offset (options) is the purchase of an equal number of identical contracts to those previously sold, resulting in no further obligation.

Ordinary Income is income from the normal activities of an individual or business, as distinguished from capital gains from the sale of assets.

Realized or *Unrealized Profit or Loss* is the profit or loss resulting from the sale of an asset. If you sell the asset at a gain, you will have a realized profit. Before you sell, your profit is unrealized.

Tax Avoidance is the reduction of a tax liability by legal means. For example, investors who itemize deductions may avoid some taxes by deducting the cost of this book and similar books.

Taxable Event, as used here, means any sale that results in a profit or loss which would affect taxes.

Unearned Income is individual income, such as dividends, investment interest, option premiums, and capital gains realized from invested capital.

The Option Income Portfolio and Taxes

Capital gains or losses can come from many sources, such as the sale of stocks, options, real estate, and other items. Once a taxable event results in a capital gain or loss, it may be included with all other capital gains and losses for tax purposes. The IRS requires you to net or offset these gains and losses against each other to produce a net capital gain or net capital loss for your tax year. Long-term and short-term gains and losses must be totaled and netted-out against each other. Your payback will be lower taxes.

Net capital losses can be used to reduce ordinary income to the extent allowed by the IRS. Capital losses can be offset dollar-for-dollar against capital gains and $3,000 of ordinary income.

The 1990 Act reinstated preferential tax treatment of long-term capital gains for certain taxpayers by fixing a "maximum" tax rate of 28% on net capital gains (net long-term capital gains minus net short-term capital losses). Thus, in some but not all cases, individual investors with profitable positions may have an incentive to hold such positions for an extended period of time.

The long-term holding period will generally be more than one year. If stock is acquired and held for more than one year, the resulting gain or loss on a sale is a long-term capital gain or loss. If the stock is purchased and sold in one year or less, any resulting gain or loss is short-term. Any congress may change these provisions.

Net capital losses (long-term as well as short-term) can be used to reduce ordinary income to the extent allowed by the IRS. The capital loss carryover can be used when you have a greater capital loss than allowed to deduct for the tax year. This excess of unused capital loss is carried-over to the next tax year. In this way accumulated capital loss can be used, even if it takes several years.

Avoid unpleasant tax surprises. Keep careful track of both gains and losses, so that there is still time for year-end transactions. If there is a net gain, it is advisable to take a year-end loss to balance against it, thus reducing or eliminating taxes.

Tax planning requires knowing where you are concerning taxes and what tax liability will be incurred from your investment transactions. Any investment strategy that ignores tax consequences is not well planned. Tax planning is for all investors, not just the wealthy, and next April 15th is not the time to do it.

Option Contract (Closing Transaction)

When an option contract (opening transaction) is sold, neither the profit or loss nor the tax consequences can be determined until the option contract ends. There are three possible outcomes:

1. *Exercise*—The holder of the option contract calls your stock away. You have to sell the stock at the strike price to which you had previously agreed.
2. *Expiration*—The holder of the option contract does not call your stock. The expiration date has passed.

3. *Purchasing an offsetting option*—Buying an option contract to close one previously sold. This closing buy ends your obligation to deliver or sell the stock.

Until the opening transaction (the selling of an option) has ended by exercise, by expiration, or by purchasing a closing offsetting transaction, the option will remain open. The premium received for writing a call is not included in income calculations until the contract has ended.

When an option is sold on stocks and it is not exercised, the premium is a short-term capital gain. If the option is exercised, the premium plus the strike price received become the sale price of the stock. The resulting gain or loss depends upon the holding period of the underlying security used to satisfy the assignment. It is possible that previously owned stock will be long-term, and thus may result in a long-term capital gain or loss.

Gain or loss on buying an option offset closes the option obligation as short-term, regardless of the length of time the call was outstanding.

Tax Deferral

Premium money received is not considered taxable until the option ends. Until that time the final outcome of the option contract cannot be determined as a capital gain or loss.

If you have stock that has appreciated in value, but want to defer the gain until the following year, consider writing an option with an expiration date next year. If the purchaser of the option doesn't exercise it until next year (or it expires), both the amount you received from selling the option and the proceeds from selling the stock are not reported until the following year.

Tax Gains or Losses

Gain or loss in some cases can be determined by the writer of options. When you have an option gain or loss, the option is treated as having been sold or exchanged on the date it ends.

For example, Pete purchased 100 shares of ABC stock for $20 per share on November 22. On December 1 the stock was selling for $50 a share, but Pete wanted to defer the gain until the following year and protect himself against a market decline. Pete wrote an option for $40 per share expiring in three months. He received $11 per share for selling this option. Pete has acquired protection against a market decline (he has $11 premium in his account). If the buyer of the option does not exercise it, Pete reports the $11 per share as a capital gain. If the option is exercised, the $11 per share is added to the $40 per share exercise price, making a total sale price of $51. A gain would have been realized when the option position was closed. Total gain is $31 ($51-$20) per share.

If the ABC stock had continued to appreciate, the option would have been exercised. Pete could have bought other shares of the stock in the open market to deliver against the call, or he could choose to prevent an exercise by purchase or buy-back of the option. A loss would have been realized when the option position was closed in either of these two ways. Buying back the offsetting option contract creates a capital loss, a taxable event. It also produces a gain in equity, which is non-taxable.

When buying new shares to deliver to an option assignment, a choice is presented. The buyer of the option does not care how long the stock was held, be it 10 years or 1 day. All the buyer wants is the stock you are obligated to deliver at the strike price. Since all common stocks are fungible, you can deliver old or newly acquired shares.

It is at this time that you can create a realized gain or loss on these shares of stock.

If the cost basis is higher than the current market price, buy new shares at the lower price and deliver the old, higher priced shares. Now you will have a lower cost basis for these shares in your portfolio and at the same time have a larger realized loss on this transaction.

If the cost basis is lower than the current market price, buy new shares at the higher price and deliver these. You will keep your lower-cost basis shares in your portfolio and avoid a capital gain, a taxable event. By delivering the new, higher priced shares you will have a larger realized loss on this transaction.

Of course, if there are capital losses to use, the lower-cost basis stock could be used for delivery in both cases, and a larger capital gain would be realized for these transactions.

Capital Loss or Gain Account

It is important to keep a running total on the capital losses or gains in your option income portfolio. Only by having this information available can it be determined which of the closing option strategies to use. If there are losses, take gains, if there are gains, take losses. Remember, capital gains plus up to $3,000 of ordinary income can be offset by capital losses dollar-for-dollar.

Make your decisions considering your total tax liability. With careful planning, you can realize long-term capital gains on one side and a short-term loss on the other.

Remember that a tax-shelter program helps to reduce, defer, or eliminate taxes on personal income. While the program offers reasonable economic gains, the first and second possible outcomes of an option are both taxable events. We retain the cash premiums after the option contract expires. The third possible outcome is not a taxable event. The unrealized gain on the increase of the stock's value is non-taxable.

There can be tax benefits when the option is exercised. The length of time you held the underlying stock decides the holding period, not the option. When you own the stock short-term, the option tax consequences are short-term. You will pay the highest tax rate for those gains or losses realized as short-term.When you own the stock long-term the option tax consequences are long-term. The premium becomes part of the selling price of the stock. It adds more net gain to the transaction (and lowers the real cost, out of pocket).

When ABC Corp. is bought in January at $20 (cost basis), the investor writes an April 20 option for a premium of 2 (the out-of-pocket cost is $18). The call is exercised in April for $20, and the profit on the ABC Corp. transaction is a $2 short-term gain. With options, the premium increases the amount realized by the writer on the sale of the underlying stock.

Now let's assume that the investor has owned ABC Corp. for a long-term holding period. In January the investor writes an April 20 option for a premium of 2. If the stock is exercised in April, the tax sale price is $22 ($20 cost plus $2 premium). The $2 profit is long-term gain.

At year-end, if the price of the stock has increased, buy back the option and take losses on this year's tax return. Sell a new option with an exercise date in the next year. This premium will not be taxable until the next year's tax return, after the option has ended. By buying back the option, you could extend the holding period of a short-term underlying stock until it becomes a long-term holding.

Taxable events can be decreased and non-taxable events increased with a high degree of control in an option income portfolio. They are an excellent means of tax-sheltered income.

Most writers in the financial press never discuss the opportunity to use exchange-traded options. This buy-back capability exists because of the OCC. You can study the mechanics in the prospectus of the OCC. The OCC makes the option contract fungible. All options for the same underlying stock, having the same exercise price and the same expiration date, are fungible, one to another.

The buying back of fungible option contracts will be done regularly, which benefits both your option income portfolio and your tax consequences.

"Patience is not only virtue, it pays."
B.C. Forbes

"The one thing that hurts more than paying an income tax is not having income to pay an income tax on."
Harvey Friedentag

CHAPTER 7

Options: Standard Operating Procedures

"The ladder of success doesn't care who climbs it."
Frank Tyger

Let us assume that you purchased 100 shares of ABC Corp., an optionable stock, for $35 a share at a total cost of $3,500 on February 21. On the same day you sold an opening option for three months to expire on May 20 at a strike price of $30, for which you received $850. On that day, your out-of-pocket cost is $3,500 - $850 = $2,650 ($26.50 a share).

This is investing without fear. Because of the option hedge, you are protected in a price decline until the stock price drops below $26.50 per share.

You know that when you buy a stock, the price can go up, go down, or stay the same. You also know that for the three-month period there will be a related price movement between the stock and the option contract that you sold.

Table 7-1 shows what can happen to the market price of the option value at expiration due to stock price movement.

Table 7-1 reflects five possible market prices for the stock on May 20. For each stock price you can see the related prices of the option contract. There is no time value remaining. The intrinsic value is zero if the stock is selling at or below the exercise price of $30. The intrinsic value is the difference between the higher stock price and the strike price.

If the option is exercised (called away), you would receive $3,000. You already received $850 for the option, or

Table 7-1

	Price Feb 21	Prices May 20 (expiration day)				
ABC Corp. Stock:	35.00	25	30	35	40	45
ABC May 30 Option:						
Intrinsic Value	5.00	0	0	5	10	15
Time Value	3.50	0	0	0	0	0
Option Value	8.50	0	0	5	10	15

total cash of $3,000 + 850 = $3,850. You paid $3,500 in stock cost. Your gross profit would be $3,850 - 3,500 = $350, not allowing for stock brokerage commissions. If called, you would have the $350 gross profit plus your original $3,500.

Your stock will not be called if the stock price is below the exercise price of $30. Stocks are rarely called during the life of a contract. Options are exercised the last few days, when the time value component of the option premium is very small.

As a rule of thumb, it is advisable to buy back your option if the price is one-half or less of the premium received, and sell a new option for the next full option expiration cycle. If it were mid-way (45 days), you could buy back the option for $1.75 resulting in your retaining $1.75, of the time value as well as the $5.00 intrinsic value. By selling the new option you bring in more new money.

No Time = No Time Value

In our example, the time value on February 21 is $3.50 per share. At expiration, the time value component of the option premium is always zero. Understanding this fact permits you to make money in your option income portfolio. You always realize the time value as a gross profit.

The opening sell is your decision. The cash received for the sale, less the commission, will be credited to your brokerage account on the next trading day. You get your money in one day, and if you just bought the stock you will have 3 business days (effective June 1, 1995) to pay for it. You will be using other people's money since the proceeds of the option sale will apply toward the purchase of the stock you just bought.

The net cash you receive from this opening sell transaction falls into the "option premiums received" category. This income increases the cash amount carried in your account. When you sell an option contract, you cannot determine the tax consequences until the option has expired in one of the three following ways:

1. Exercise—the owner of the option calls the stock away.
2. Expiration—the option may expire worthless with the passage of time.
3. Buy-back—when the option is bought back with a closing buy, it eliminates the obligation to deliver or sell the stock.

There are three ways to create a taxable event:

1. Exercise—you cannot overrule.
2. Expiration—you cannot hold back.
3. Buy-back—buying back your option contract is something you certainly decide.

Most professionals will promote waiting until expiration if the option is not exercised, totally ignoring the buy-back method.

In the example of the three month ABC May 30 option, on May 20, no option holder would force you to sell the stock, since the stock was under the $30 strike price. Clearly the same shares could be had for less on the open market.

At expiration, what action would you take if ABC Corp. stock was trading at one of five closing prices: 25, 30, 35, 40, and 45?

If the stock price is at or below the strike price of 30, you take no action. The option contract will expire worthless. This expiration is a taxable event.

If the stock price at expiration is above the strike price of 30, and if you wish to keep the stock, buy the offsetting option contract with a closing buy. Do this just before expiration, at the prices illustrated in the total option value row in Table 7-1. On May 20, with the stock price at $35, you would pay $35 - $30 = $5 to buy the option back. At $40 you would pay $40 - $30 = $10. And at $45 you would pay $45 - $30 = $15.

To take these actions, instruct your stockbroker to "buy one ABC Corp. May 30 to close at the market." Any one of these closing buy transactions is a taxable event.

What Can Happen After the Option

To explain tax implications further, lets look at the three things a stock can do after you optioned it: go down, go up, or stay the same.

Stock Price Goes Down

Let's consider a worst-case scenario. ABC Corp. stock declines from your purchase price of $35 (February 21) to $25 a share on May 20. (The very worst case would be if the company went broke and its stock fell to zero.) Remember, diversify your portfolio to minimize the risk of a bankrupt stock.

In this example the tax consequences are not good. There is a realized capital gain of $8.50 taxable as ordinary income. The unrealized capital loss in the stock of -$10 per share is a reduction in your equity. The only comfort is the pre-tax hedge given to you by your receipt of the cash option premium of $8.50. This cash flow reduced your pre-tax loss in equity to -$1.50 when the stock value went down $10.

This stock is only 1 of some 20 stocks you should own in your option income portfolio. You would expect to have some short-term losses from other options that you sold then bought back at higher prices. These net realized capital losses can be applied against the $8.50 net capital gain you received.

Clearly, buying stock at $35 and selling options for $8.50 is a more conservative way to own stock than simply purchasing stock and then waiting for its market price to rise. On a pre-tax cash basis, your invested capital would not be reduced until the stock price declined from $35 (your cost basis) to $26.50, a 24% decline.

Stock Price Stays the Same

If the stock price on May 20 was $35, the same you paid, you would pay $5 to buy the option offset. You would then have a net realized gain of $3.50, taxable as ordinary income. You would have no change in unrealized gain for the stock itself. Let's see how you did, when the stock price remains unchanged.

Strike Price	Today's Stock Price	Option Premium	Today's Stock Price	Options per Year	Annualized %
$30	$35	+ $8.50	÷ $35	× 4	= 40%

With the stock price unchanged we made 10% in three months and 40% annualized, before commissions. Not bad!

Stock Price Goes Up

Despite how high the stock price may go, you agreed to sell your stock for $30. Actually you are selling for the $30 strike price plus the $8.50 option premium.

Let's consider the net effect of buying back the option offset when the stock price is above the strike price (when the option is trading in-the-money). When you buy the option offset, your obligation to sell stock at the exercise price has been canceled. Using the new, higher market value of your stock, sell a higher strike price option.

If the stock price on May 20 is 45, you will pay $15 for the option buy-back (option offset). This produces a realized short-term capital loss of $6.50 ($15 - $8.50 = -$6.50). Your unrealized capital gain in your underlying stock becomes $10 ($35 up to $45). You have an unrealized gain of $10 in your equity and a realized loss of $6.50.

What you have done is shift assets from one position to another. You picked up a non-taxable equity gain and realized a tax loss benefit.

In rising markets you will generate year-to-year tax loss carry-overs, normally short-term. Any unused capital loss remaining after taking the maximum deduction allowable against ordinary income can be carried over indefinitely until used. Many investors build a loss carry-over account, which allows them to realize tax-free cash in the future. Gains realized on a future trade can be offset by losses in the loss carry-over account.

This loss carry-over account is valuable because it comes from your option buy-back activities, which can produce non-taxable gains in your portfolio. You actually gain equity while receiving a short-term tax loss. You make money while generating a tax deduction!

An option being exercised may be to your advantage. If you wish to sell the underlying stock at expiration, you simply do nothing. When it is in-the-money it will be called. This is a welcome exercise that you control.

I sell an option deep in-the-money knowing that it will be called. It usually does the trick. If the stock should drop below the strike price, after writing it deep in-the-money, you can keep a large premium and do it again.

The welcome exercise is of greater value because of the favorable tax treatment of capital gains. Normally cash option premiums are short-term gains. When the underlying stock is called away, the option premium received assumes the status of the stock's long- or short-term characteristic.

The adjusted sales basis of the stock called away is the strike price plus the call option premium. If the stock is a long-term holding, the option premium will be considered a long-term holding. This gives you the opportunity to turn a short-term capital gain (the option premium) into a long-term holding for tax purposes.

The unwelcome exercise happens suddenly. You receive an unplanned demand from the holder of the option to exercise his right to buy your stock at the agreed upon strike price. You do not have any control of the unwelcome assignment. OCC procedures require that on the same day you are called or assigned, you must comply with the terms of the option contract. You must sell the stock.

Notice I said *you must comply* with the option holder's request and deliver stock. It does not have to be your shares—just the same number of shares for the same strike price.

Whether the exercise against you is welcome or not, it is essential that you understand that in responding to an exercise you do not have to sell your originally optioned shares. Your choice is to deliver shares you already own or to buy and deliver new shares purchased on the open market at the prevailing price. Selling the new shares to the option holder at the strike price fulfills the terms of the contract, using fungibility.

This will be easier to understand if we return to the last trades with ABC Corp. On February 21 you bought 100 shares of ABC Corp. at $35 and on the same day sold an option (ABC Corp. May 30 for $8.50). On May 20 the ABC Corp. stock is selling for $45 and your broker informs you that your 100 shares of ABC Corp. stock was exercised for $30. You can make one of two decisions.

You can decide to retain your shares. For whatever reason, you do not want to sell them. Maybe you want to hold them long enough to realize a long-term capital gain. Another consideration is that the stock has gone up from $35 to $45 a share, and you would prefer to keep the lower cost shares in your portfolio and avoid a taxable event if possible. You bought the shares at $35. You wrote the call for $8.50. Now you have been assigned at $30. The tax implications are: -$35 + $8.50 +$30 = +$3.50 × 100 = $350.00 short-term taxable capital gain.

You can decide to buy new shares at $45 and sell these for $30 in cash. You write the option for $8.50 to sell stock for $30 and buy stock to deliver at $45. The tax implications are: +$8.50 +$30 -$45 = -$6.50 X 100 = - $650 short-term capital loss.

Cost Basis of 100 ABC Corp. at $35	$3,500
Market Value of 100 ABC Corp. at $45	4,500
Gain in Stock Value (non-taxable)	1,000
Short-Term Capital loss (deductible)	-650
Net After-Tax Gain	$350

You receive a net non-taxable gain of $350, 10% in 90 days on your equity of $3,500. Plus your tax savings are used at tax time. Your annualized, after-tax return on your applied equity is 40%. Note that the gain in equity resulted from the time value of the cash option premium at the time of your opening-sell.

There has been no decrease in your equity by these trades, because you owned the underlying stock. Your after-tax equity increased. As part of the transactions, you obtained a realized short-term capital loss. These losses from option buy-backs may be accumulated during the tax year. If you do not use all the losses in one year, you may carry the unused losses to later tax years. Such totaled option buy-back losses become the source of the tax-loss carry-over account discussed previously. We are realizing tax losses without equity losses. The second decision was to buy 100 shares of ABC Corp. at $45, a $4,500 cash outlay. You sold these 100 shares of ABC Corp. at $30, or $3,000. This totals to -$15 dollars (-$45 +$30 = -$15); you paid out $1,500 in cash. Your cost basis of the stock is 45 and your sale basis of the stock is 30, a net loss of $1,500.

The sale of the ABC Corp. in response to an option assignment creates a taxable event by closing the formerly open position of your option contract. IRS rules require that you increase your sale basis ($30) by the cash option premium you received for selling the opening transaction ($8.50). In this example your adjusted sales basis is $30 plus $8.50, equaling $38.50. You sold the stock for a loss of $15 per share and received $8.50 for the option, so you lost $6.50 per share. The out-of-pocket loss is $650. Your equity has increased more than enough to cover this amount.

The loss for tax purposes is your cost basis ($45 minus your adjusted sale basis of $38.50). This produces a net realized short-term loss (-$45 +$38.50 = -$6.50). This loss is exactly what the loss would have been if you had done the option buy-back.

Your decision was to keep your original stock and buy and sell the new stock on the same day. You have a gain and tax situation that is the same as though you had used the option buy-back offset. Common stock commissions are somewhat larger than option commissions. Thus, the unwelcome option assignment is slightly more costly than the option buy-back offset.

Buying new shares when you are exercised (either welcome or unwelcome) gives you the opportunity of selling the higher price shares to the option holder. In this example the new shares were higher, so we sold the new shares and kept our lower cost basis. If our cost basis in the original shares was higher, we would sell the older, higher cost shares and retain the newer, lower cost shares in our portfolio.

Remember, if you sell options on shares of stock that you have held for years, and your cost basis is very low, you can always substitute newly acquired shares to comply with the terms of the option contract. You never have to sell your original, low-cost basis shares in response to an unwelcome assignment.

Since earlier you had declined decision one, and now you must give an order to your broker. "Buy 100 ABC Corp. at the market and sell those shares just purchased at $30 to satisfy the assignment I have received."

Now that you have satisfied the call, the underlying stock in your possession is available for writing again. Any stock that went up 28% in three months has caught the eye of the speculators. If you wrote the next period (August calls), and wrote it in-the-money as before, you would get a rich premium. The ABC Corp. August 40 probably would bring in $5 for intrinsic value and $4.50 for time value, you probably would get $9.50, or $950, which more than offsets óur previous $650 loss.

Selling and Buying Back Calls, One Stock for One Year

To obtain the best results, all blocks of stock should be working for you at all times. Therefore, upon closing an option on a block of stock, you simultaneously sell to open another, using a *spread order*. A spread order is similar in action to a buy/write, as both sides of the transaction have to be completed or the order will not be executed.

Table 7-2 is a simulation of potential results of an XYZ Co. The purpose is to show the type of results obtained from fluctuating stock prices and actions.

Simultaneously using a spread order, we wrote the July 17 1/2 options at 1 3/4 to net $875. In May we bought these back at 1 3/4 for a profit of $500.

We continued to sell and buy back until November. Then, anxious to set up a tax loss, we bought back the January 15 options at a cost of $4, or $2,000, for a short-term loss of $500. This would be applicable against other income. The same day we recouped the dollar loss by selling 5 April 15 options with a spread order.

Table 7-2

500 shares of XYZ Co. Market price at the beginning of the year: $20

Date	Action	Income	Cost	P/L
1/15	expired 5 Jan 22 1/2	1,100*		
1/15	sold 5 Apr 20 @ 2	1,000		
3/3	bought 5 Apr 20 @ 1/2		-250	750
3/3	sold 5 Jul 17 1/2 @1 3/4	875		
5/24	bought 5 Jul 17½ @ 3/4		-375	500
5/24	sold 5 Oct 17½ @1 3/4	875		
6/22	bought 5 Oct 17½ @ 1/2		-250	625
6/22	sold 5 Jan 17½ @1 3/4	875		
8/23	bought 5 Jan 17½ @ 1/2		-250	625
8/23	sold 5 Jan 15 @3	1,500		
11/29	bought 5 Jan 15 @4		-2,000	-500
11/29	sold 5 Apr 15 @4**	2,000		
	Total	6,125	-3,125	3,000

*Last year's option expired this year.
**Next year's settlement
In addition, there were $300 in annual dividends.

At year end, the price of the stock was at $15. We had a paper loss of $2,500, but we had received $6,125 income and spent $3,125, for a net profit of $3,000. If we had not taken a loss our total return would have been higher. Without the tax loss our taxes would have been greater, because all gains, with all options, are short-term.

Option Income Portfolio of Actual Transactions

Table 7-3 illustrates the operational ideas we have covered. It shows the actual transactions made in my option income portfolio from 8-27-90 to 5-9-91. All dollar amounts have been rounded, including sales commissions. Remember, the margin interest and commissions are paid by the dividends generated from the stocks in the account.

Schering Plough Corp. stock came into my portfolio in 1986 when it bought out Key Pharmaceutical. I originally found Key on the option page in January 1984, and it was a good write. After further study I decided it was an excellent underlying stock to hold. In February 1984, with a buy/write order to my broker, I bought 500 shares at $11 and simultaneously wrote options. In September 1984, the stock price dropped to a new low and I reacted. I bought back the November 10 calls and also I bought 500 more shares at $9. This lowered my net cost per share from $11 to $10 (500 at $11 and 500 at $9; $5,500 + $4,500 = $10,000 for 1,000 shares, or $10 per share).

The 1,000 shares of Key in the stock swap became 342 shares of Schering Plough in 1986. I sold the 42 shares at $36 since only round lots can be used to do options. I always try to keep equal amounts of money invested in my option income portfolio, around $10,000 per company. I had 300 shares at $36 each to equal $10,800.

Schering Plough prospered through the next few years. They had two stock splits of 2-for-1. The first gave me a total of 600 shares and the second split gave me a total of 1,200 shares. The dividends increased each year as well.

Now on to the period I am using for this illustration. On 8-27-90, I wrote an option for Schering Plough February 45, when the market price was $47, and received $4 for each of my 1,200 shares ($4,800).

The cash option premium received on 8-27-90 was taxed as 1991 income since the option expired in February 1991. I got the use of the money in August 1990, though the taxes were not payable until 1992. How's that for a tax deferment?

On 1-8-91 the market price of the stock was $40.50. With a spread order I bought back the call for $0.75, a total of $900. $4,800 -$900 = a $3,900 capital gain. I sold 12 May 45 calls for $1.875 each = $2,250. I never hold stock without writing options. Yes, the stock could go up and I could option it for more money, but it could go down and I would

---

Table 7-3

Selling and Buying Calls for One Year: Schering Plough
Total shares owned: 1,200

Date	Price	Market Action	Income	Cost	P/L
8/27	47.00	sold 12 Feb 45 @ 4	4,800		
1/8	40.50	bought 12 Feb 45 @ 3/4		900	3,900
		sold 12 May 45 @ 1 7/8	2,250		
5/9	53.50	bought 12 May 45 @ 8 3/8		10,050	-7,800
		sold 12 Nov 50 @ 6*	7,200		
		Total	14,250	10,950	-3,900

*Settlement after August (one-year period).

---

get less. Believe me, it is better to write the option on your stock and watch it go up than not to write the option and watch your stock go down.

This stock did go up, and how! The market price of Schering Plough went to $53.50. I knew I would be exercised shortly as it was a May call. I wanted to keep my low-cost basis in the stock. On 5-9-91, using a spread order, I bought back, closing 12 contracts of Schering Plough May 45, for intrinsic value only, at $8.375, a total of $10,050. The -$7,800 short-term capital loss ($2,250 - $10,050) went into my capital loss account to be used against other income in my portfolio.

I had only $10,800 cost basis in the Schering Plough stock and put in an additional $7,800. You may feel that putting in an additional $7,800 to buy back the expiring May 45 call is risky business. Surely, a stock that can rise rapidly from $40.50 to $53.50 from January to May (four months), can fall just as fast.

With the spread order I made an opening-sell to provide some money to offset part of the $7,800 May buy-back, and to provide a partial, risk-reducing hedge against a stock decline from the new high of $53.50. My point is, it is unlikely that anyone would commit $7,800 for the buy-back without the availability of a cash infusion from the new opening-sale. By selling 12 contracts of Schering Plough November 50 at $6, I received $7,200 to go against that loss. My cash outlay at this point was $600. The debit balance in my margin account had increased by $600. For this $600 debit I realized a capital loss of $7,800, to be used in offsetting other income in the account. Any loss remaining can offset up to $3,000 of ordinary earned income. In this example the option loss was $7,800. This was a realized short-term capital loss. It was also a non-equity loss. I did not lose $7,800—I did not lose anything. I made money in the related transactions, including income-tax savings. Taken together, this realized capital loss has a value, at the 25% income tax level, of $1,950 in tax savings.

By doing the last transaction I have taken the value of Schering Plough shares from $45 to $50 per share, or 1,200 × $5 = $6,000. *In my option income portfolio, I now own 1,200 shares of Schering Plough with a strike price of $50 per share, or 1,200 × $50 = $60,000.*

The share price of Schering Plough could drop from $50 to $44 before I would begin to lose equity ($50 - $6 = $44). The share price could rise from $50 to $56 before I would begin to lose the upside price movement ($50 + $6 = $56). With the use of options I am protected up or down from $56 to $44. It is a safe, secure, and profitable feeling to have this protection. This is truly investing without fear.

I had been working on this book for many months, during which time the May 91 transactions took place. I did not plan the above scenario, nor could I. You have to learn to react to the irrational market system and use it to your advantage. The subject of reducing and controlling risk to the portfolio is the theme of this book.

"Give me the luxuries of life and I will willingly do without the necessities."
Frank Lloyd Wright

"What we call luck is simply pluck, and doing things over and over; Courage and will, perseverance and skill, are the four leaves of luck's clover."
The Four Leaf Clover, Unknown

CHAPTER 8

Long-Term Equity Anticipation Securities (LEAPS)

*"Money doesn't bring happiness,
but it calms the nerves."*
French Proverb

In the 1929 Crash people really did leap from rooftops. What a twist that now the latest options being sold are called LEAPS—Long-term Equity Anticipation Securities.

Long-term options add a whole, unprecedented range of option possibilities, many suited for low-budget investors. The LEAPS concept can also captivate resourceful stock owners as a result of the similarities between LEAPS and stocks and because of the more conservative nature afforded LEAPS by their long-term expirations.

LEAPS provide an investment vehicle that permits option trading with as little as 100 shares of stock. Trading in regular stock options would not be possible because of the commission cost, which would eat up all of the premium. The greater time premium with LEAPS enables one to follow the principles of investing without fear with one round lot!

LEAPS are long-term options available on approximately 150 well-known, blue-chip stocks of companies with large capitalization. LEAPS began trading on October 5, 1990. They enable the owner of the underlying stock to sell an option with an expiration up to three years in the future. LEAPS options expire in January of the specific year. Investors find the longer maturities provide the additional time for investment forecasts to materialize. Daily time decay is less significant than for a short-term option.

The combination of long-time expiration and the consequent high-dollar premiums relative to shorter-term options confounds conventional option analysis. Talk about time value—20 to 30% of the stock price! The higher time value premium reduces the chance of early exercise, because of the cost to buy a LEAPS versus an option call with a few months left.

"Take the money and run."
American Dictum

An investor can get a fairly high time-value premium when writing out-of-the-money LEAPS calls. LEAPS allow more time for the stock to appreciate, thereby generating additional profits—limited to the strike price of the option. In the event of a stock price decline, again from the high time-value premium, there will be greater protection, although still limited, against loss. Neither of these two conditions would be present with ordinary options. The result is that the option writing technique is safer with LEAPS.

A good way for an investor to start safely is with the purchase of 100 shares of a blue-chip stock and the sale of a LEAPS contract with a large premium for time. Until the introduction of this option, I had a problem suggesting how an investor with limited capital could get started in my program.

Buying one blue-chip stock and receiving a large cash premium up front does not diversify a portfolio. However, LEAPS work using all the other operating methods discussed in this book.

Writing high-cash premium LEAPS gives much downside protection and provides attractive returns to maturity, whether called or not. For conservative investors in dividend-paying blue-chip stocks, selling LEAPS options is a viable, attractive strategy.

Of course, you should still add additional funds to your account, as it is your goal to become diversified as soon as possible. A second LEAPS in a different equity is a start. This will be quickly done by using additional funding, the cash premium and dividends, which you should invest in a brokerage cash account which draws money market interest.

> *"Success is a science. If you create*
> *the conditions you get the results."*
> Oscar Wilde

Buy Stock/Sell LEAPS Strategy

The buy stock/sell LEAPS strategy, also known as a covered write, reduces the risk of stock ownership by making the option income portfolio less susceptible to short-term market moves. Writing in-the-money LEAPS offers greater downside protection and less incremental increase than writing out-of-the-money LEAPS. The total return approach to LEAPS writing attempts to strike a balance between downside protection and income from premiums, stock ownership, and dividends. This balance is usually realized by writing LEAPS that are slightly in- or out-of-the-money.

Investors write LEAPS calls for three primary reasons:

1. To realize additional return on the underlying stock.
2. To gain some protection from a decline in stock price.
3. To use less of their money initially to purchase stock by doing a buy/write. Stock price minus the LEAPS premium for time value equals the breakeven point.

Covered LEAPS writing will outperform outright stock ownership if the stock falls, remains the same, or rises less than the premium received.

Leaps Examples

The following analysis draws on data in tables 8-1 and 8-2.

Table 8-1: Some Equity LEAPS Available For Trading August 1994

Company	Symbol	Company	Symbol
Abbott Labs	ABT	AMR Corp	AMR
AT&T	T	AmerBarck	ABX
American Exp	AXP	American Home	AHP
Amgen Inc	AMGN	Apple Comp	APCI
Bank America	BAC	Bell South	BLS
Blockbuster	BBEC	Boeing Co	BA
Bristol-Myer	BMY	Centocor Inc	COQ
Chase Man	CMB	Citicorp	CCI
Coca-Cola Co	KO	Compaq Comp	CPQ
Delta Air Lines	DAL	Digital Equip	EC
Disney (Walt)	DIS	Dow Chemical	DOW
Eastman Kodak	EK	Exxon Corp	XON
Federal Nat M	FNM	Ford Motor Co	F
Gap Inc	GPS	General Elec	GE
General Motors	GM	Georgia-Pacific	GP
Glaxo Holdings	GLX	GTE Corp	GTE
H.J. Heinz Co	HNZ	Home Depot	HD
IBM	IBM	Intel Corp	ITEL
Johns & Johns	JNJ	K Mart Corp	KM
The Limited Inc	LTD	Liz Claiborne	LIZ
McDonald's Corp	MCD	Merk & Co Inc	MRK
Microsoft Corp	MSFT	Mobil Corp	MOB
Monsanto Co	MTC	Motorola Inc	MOT
Oracle Systems	ORQ	PepsiCo Inc	PEP
Pfizer Inc	PFE	Philip Morris	MO
Proctor & Gamble	PG	RJR Nabisco	RN
Sears Roebuck	S	Texas Inst	TXN
Triton Energy	OIL	UAL Corp	UAL
Union Carbide	UK	Unisys Corp	UIS
Upjohn Co	UPJ	US West	USW
Wal-Mart	WMT	Waste Manage	WMX
Westinghouse El	WX	Xerox Corp	XRX

Table 8-2: Some Sample LEAPS
Available August 19, 1994

Stock	Price	LEAPS	Strike	Premium	Strike & Premium over Stock Price
Amgen	55 1/4	Jan 96	60	8 1/2	13.25
AT&T	53 1/8	Jan 96	60	3 1/4	10.12
AppleC	34 7/8	Jan 96	40	5 1/4	10.37
Chrysl	47 3/8	Jan 96	60	3 1/4	15.87
DuPont	58 1/2	Jan 96	70	2 5/8	14.12
GM	50 1/4	Jan 96	65	3	17.75
IBM	68 1/8	Jan 96	80	4 3/4	16.62
Merck	34	Jan 96	40	2 3/16	8.18
PhilMr	55 1/4	Jan 96	60	4 1/2	9.25
RJR Nb	6 1/8	Jan 96	7 1/2	1	2.38
WestEl	12 1/8	Jan 96	15	1 5/16	4.32
WestEl	12 1/8	Jan 97	15	2	4.48

IBM

With IBM, a higher dollar cost stock, we have used a buy write—100 shares of IBM were purchased at $68 1/8 ($6,812) and one contract of the IBM January 1996 80 LEAPS was sold. The 4 3/4 cash premium ($475) protects down to $63.37. The strike price is $80, which means that if the option is exercised the stock will be sold for $8,000. The total of the value rise in the stock sale price over the stock purchase price plus the premium is $11.88, or $1,188. In addition there would have been 6 dividends of $25.00 bringing the total to $2,300 on an investment of $5,262—about 44%. In order to keep the stock with its lower cost basis if the stock goes up above the $80 strike price, purchase a closing option and immediately sell a new LEAPS opening transaction at a higher strike price, taking in a new cash premium to help finance the buy-back.

If the market price of the IBM stock goes down before January 1996, buy an option offset and cancel the obligation. Immediately sell another LEAPS option at a lower strike price, taking in a new cash premium.

If the market price of the IBM stock stays the same until January 1996, let the LEAPS contract expire worthless. At this point the return would be $475 (cash premium) plus $150 (dividends) for a total return of about 11% on a flat investment. The non-LEAPS owner of a flat investment would only have the dividends, about a 2% return. At expiration sell another LEAPS option at the same strike price, taking in a new cash premium.

RJR Nabisco

With RJR Nabisco, a lower dollar cost stock, we have used a buy write—500 shares of RJR Nabisco were purchased at 6 1/8 ($3,062) and 5 contracts of the January 1996 7 1/2 LEAPS were sold. The $1 cash premium ($500) protects down to 5 1/8. The strike price is $7.50, which means that if the option is exercised the stock will be sold for $3,750. The total of the value rise in the stock sale price over the stock purchase price plus the premium is $2.36, or $1,180. There would be no dividends, unless one is declared. This is an investment gain of $1,180—about 38%. In order to keep the stock with its lower cost basis if the stock goes up above the $7.50 strike price, purchase a closing option and immediately sell a new RJR Nabisco LEAPS opening transaction at a higher strike price, taking in a new cash premium to help finance the buy-back.

If the market price of the RJR Nabisco stock goes down before January 1996, buy an option offset and cancel the obligation. Immediately sell another LEAPS option at a lower strike price, taking in a new cash premium. If the market price of the stock stays the same until January 1996, let the LEAPS contract expire worthless. At this point the return would be $500 (cash premium) for a total return of about 16% on a flat investment. The non-LEAPS owner of a flat investment would have nothing for his time. At expiration sell another RJR Nabisco LEAPS option at the same strike price, taking in a new cash premium.

Westinghouse: A Longer-Term LEAPS

With Westinghouse, a moderate dollar cost stock, we have used a buy/write—500 shares of Westinghouse were purchased at 12 1/8 ($6,062) and 5 contracts of the Westinghouse January 1997 15 LEAPS were sold. The $2 cash premium ($1,000) protects down to 10 1/8. The strike price is $15, which means that if the option is exercised the stock will be sold for $7,500. The total of the value rise in the stock sale price over the stock purchase price plus the premium is $4.88, or $2,440. In addition there would have been 10 dividends of $50 ($500), bringing the total to $2,940 on an investment of $6,060—about 48%. In order to keep the stock with its lower cost basis if the stock goes up above the $15 strike price, purchase a closing option and immediately sell a new Westinghouse LEAPS opening transaction at a higher strike price, taking in a new cash premium to help finance the buy-back.

If the market price of the Westinghouse stock goes down before January 1997, buy an option offset and cancel the obligation. Immediately sell another LEAPS option at a lower strike price, taking in a new cash premium.

If the market price of the Westinghouse stock stays the same until January 1997, let the LEAPS contract expire worthless. At this point the return would be $1,000 (cash premium) plus $500 (dividends), for a total return of about 25% on a flat investment. The non-LEAPS owner of a flat investment would only have the dividends, about an 8% return. At expiration sell another Westinghouse LEAPS option at the same strike price, taking in a new cash premium.

LEAPS create exciting, new money-making opportunities for investors to achieve their intermediate-term trading goals by receiving the large time premiums. You will learn to *react* to the market. Instead of doing shorter three-month options you will be doing longer options—up to three years. Your annualized premium will be less than with short-term option contracts, but you will find that investing without fear is possible, even with a smaller investment.

> *"If a man empties his purse into his head,*
> *no one can take it away from him."*
> Benjamin Franklin

> *"Italians come to ruin most generally in three*
> *ways—women, gambling and farming.*
> *My family chose the slowest one."*
> Pope John XXIII

CHAPTER **9**

Conclusions

*"One can survive everything
nowadays except death."*
Oscar Wilde

Your reason for investing is to make money. Successful investing is like marshaling forces on a battlefield; all the pieces must work together. Tactics that are misguided can produce chaos over a long period of time. Well thought-out plans and goals and discipline can be undermined by investing in the wrong stock at the wrong time, or by dollars lost through taxes and inflation.

You must be businesslike in your investing. In spite of running successful businesses, some capable businesspeople operate their investment portfolios with complete disregard to sound business principles and practices. Trying to make profits from investing is a business venture that requires the use of accepted principles and practices.

Know what you are doing. Know as much about investing as you know about the business in which you made your original capital. Remember, if you lose your money you must spend time to re-earn it.

Operate your investment business yourself. Have the conviction of your knowledge. If you have formed a decision based on the facts, and you know that your judgment is sound, act on it. If you make a decision and fail to promptly act on it you lose both your time and the opportunity!

You are neither right nor wrong if the crowd disagrees with you. You are right because your research and reasoning are right. It is not what you think about a stock, it is what you know about a stock.

> *"Do not follow where the path may lead . . .*
> *go instead where there is no path*
> *and leave a trail."*
> Anonymous

The main principle of investing in the stock market is to never put your money in just one company. Choose carefully. Spread your risk over a portfolio of stocks. You must do your homework before you invest. Become an authority on options before you sell any. There is no substitute for knowledge: it is both power and security.

To be sure, we cannot possibly know all the ins and outs of investment markets. Most of us made our money making products or selling services. Making money with money is an art that has to be learned—often the hard way.

Fear, Greed, Hope, and One's Self

What prohibits us from approaching investing systematically, applying all of the lessons learned from our past mistakes?

The answer stems from the same elusive reason we break New Year's resolutions, have extra helpings when on a diet, and never get around to fixing that leaky faucet—human nature. The greatest obstacle to successful investing is one's lack of discipline and failure to act.

Failing to control emotions causes one to keep a losing position too long, take profits too early, or take advice from uninformed people. Two enemies of the average investor are fear and hope. They are usually accompanied by another—greed. Controlling these hindrances to success, which exist in varying degrees within all of us, is essential for successful investing.

With control of emotion and investment knowledge you will not merely hold your position, but make major capital gains. Remember, investments are good in any economic climate. You need not fear during a panic or market crash. You can make opportunities of panics and crashes by understanding their nature. You can avoid the mental upset and the emotional trauma if you grasp the patterns and learn the clues. You can preserve your capital while those around you are selling in fear when they should be buying, or buy in confidence in a declining market.

Follow these simple guidelines and you'll develop the traits of winner.

- Pay attention to the market. Scrutinize daily market prices, news, and trends.
- Have adequate capital to absorb reasonable losses.
- Maintain long-term purchasing power in your margin account.
- React to the market and the buy/sell signals with no hesitation or emotion—be disciplined.
- Diversify. Trade 15 to 25 varied industries; never more than two companies in the same group.
- Establish a well-tested long-term trading system for profit.
- Keep up with the latest information. Have reliable current sources for research.
- Avoid margin calls—always!
- Plan a strategy. Develop sound business practices. Cut losses and let profits run. Always look for a bargain undervalued stock.
- Control Risk. Use option selling for protective hedges on all equity positions in the account.
- React promptly on market knowledge.

These characteristics are important in achieving success in the option markets. Nothing prevents laypeople from acquiring the traits of a winners. Do the opposite of these characteristics and you'll be developing the traits of the loser.

The Surprising New Shape of the Economy

America has entered a period dramatically different from anything it has experienced. Critical economic forces are now reshaping both the United States and the world at large:

- long-term inflation, a rise in isolationism, resentment of the wealthy and powerful, and a lack of political resolve to control Federal deficits;
- a rebirth in U.S. technological innovation and ability to compete;
- massive restructuring of industry and banking, plus the North American Free Trade Agreement;
- the globalization of communications, technology, finance, and the stock markets; and
- the rise of capitalism and democracy in place of the discredited and crumbling tenets of communism.

As a result, the decades ahead will not resemble any other. The alleged economic recovery has no parallel in American history, and neither will the performance of the stock market.

There are two schools of thought making up conventional wisdom. One holds that the sluggish recovery will be followed by a traditional boom in which inflation and interest rates will rise. The other forecasts a depression because of excessive debt levels, weak monetary growth, and lack of responsible decisions and actions concerning governmental fiscal matters.

However, I feel that neither of these extremes—boom or bust—is likely. We will not experience a return of the 1970's inflation nor the 1930's deflation. Something very different and more subtle is already unfolding.

It is a world of low inflation, relative price shifts, and restructured industries and financial institutions.

It is not surprising then that so few people understand what is happening behind the misleading Government statistics. The statistics measure yesterday's economy—not tomorrow's, upon which the stock market is focused.

Most "experts" see the future in terms of the past. They cannot make the creative leap required to envision a totally new kind of economy. Instead they fall back on the old, traditional formulas and models because it is easier.

Investors, too, will be confused by unfamiliar signals and led into dangerous, expensive traps. Consider, for example, the dramatic rise in stock prices since October 1990 in the face of largely negative signals from the economy. Most investors were unprepared for and have been puzzled by the pattern of stock and bond prices. They have been constantly warned by the bears that stocks were too expensive, interest rates would rise, and a depression would occur.

Expensive stock prices are not a sufficient reason for turning bearish, particularly at the beginning of a cyclical bull market. The key is in understanding the trend of valuation. Stocks have achieved a record "overvaluation," and even higher levels are possible. The dangers are enormous because high stock prices always lead to big shakeouts.

"We are continually faced by great opportunities brilliantly disguised as insoluble problems."
Lee Iacoca

1994–The Madness of Crowds Returns

Where will investors' money go? Return on money market funds are now very disappointing. Meanwhile, confidence in the stock market has returned, so individual investors are likely to continue to build the equity portions of their portfolios. This phenomenon will further fuel the already evolving stock market mania for the 1990s.

For the first time in history there is more money invested in mutual funds than on deposit in the banking system.

But there is danger: when people exaggerate the significance of such events and succumb to excessive optimism, as witnessed in the '20s and '60s, prices are driven to overvaluation extremes. Panics and crashes will always follow. (*Extraordinary Popular Delusions and the Madness of Crowds* is an important work in this regard—see the Bibliography.)

Such instability and volatility will be prevalent throughout the '90s. Could the market double? Most people saw the October '87 crash as the end of a major bull market. I believe that there is compelling evidence that the crash was merely a pause in a long-term, super-cyclical mania.

Ultimately, like all madness, it will blow itself out. But before that happens, wise investors will have the opportunity to reap enormous profits.

Investors who wish to profit from the mania should heed three important lessons:

1. When stocks are moving from under- to over-valuation, total returns are so high that a fully invested position strategy will almost certainly produce superior returns compared with a market timing approach.
2. Contrary to popular belief, stocks can be good investments even when they are expensive as long as the trend to overvaluation is intact. But when

they are overvalued and the correction has begun, those stocks must be sold.

3. Money and inflation trends are critical. The ideal breeding ground for a mania is when inflation is falling and money growth is accelerating. Liquidity, rather than business activity and general prices, then pushes up stock prices.

Surprisingly, even during manias, most investors lose money! Why? Because they cannot cope with the high level of volatility and risk that is an inherent element of the mania climate. However, investors who understand the mania process and who can follow a sound strategy can capitalize on a unique opportunity.

Note well that a long-term, non-speculative, disciplined strategy is essential. To endure the high volatility possible in any mania environment requires patience and determination.

Investing Without Fear—Options has described a demonstrated, superior strategy which has rewarded those investors who followed its reasoning with higher profits by helping to minimize their risk and fear.

We have looked at the essential principles of investing and the advanced application of these ideas. If you expect to succeed you must have a goal, a plan, and discipline. Lack of any one of these will seriously hamper any investments you may make.

> *"No one can predict to what heights*
> *you can soar . . . even you will not know*
> *until you spread your wings."*
> Anonymous

There will be times when everything goes right (like Monday, October 19, 1987) presenting a buying opportunity of a lifetime, and there will be disasters when nothing goes right. Everything cycles.

The only way to tell if you are getting anywhere in the long run is to see how you are progressing on the road to your target. So, if you are really serious about this business, the first thing you have to do is establish goals and objectives. Then plan how to reach them.

There are two types investors. One type knows where their tennis balls are at any one time, and they are always looking for more return, more bounce for their dollars. They read the financial press diligently and study and understand the annual and quarterly reports. They go to stockholder meetings if possible. Their favorite TV station is CNBC, the financial channel. They know the ticker symbols of their stocks and options, and like to trade them. To them this isn't work—it's fun. It is a hobby, business, and good sex all mixed together. It fills much (or all) of their spare time. Their friends are from the investment world, and they never tire of talking stock market with each other. Most of them do pretty well in their investment activities.

Most, though aren't like this. They either totally ignore investments or view them as a necessary evil. They become slightly interested in developing and maintaining an investment program, but fail to sustain that interest. It is a confusing and intimidating world out there. It is little wonder that most of them prefer to spend their spare time on something they really enjoy.

If you are the second type, there is good news. You don't have to spend much time and effort to establish and maintain a sound option income portfolio program. Once committed, all you have to do is keep a supervisory eye over the whole process.

You have to manage your money. Although it does take time and attention, it just isn't that difficult. Once you have established a planned program it should not amount to more than two or three hours a week. We have found that the vast majority of investors can easily manage a personal investment program with very little guidance from outside sources. It requires reading the financial pages of your daily paper and the business reports mailed by the companies in which you own shares, and occasionally calling your broker. It doesn't require riding a roller coaster of emotion and fear as the financial markets cycle. It permits you to view Black Monday with a serene detachment. This simplicity is crucial.

By going for the long-term, the small investor frees himself from the day-to-day market frenzies that lead to whipsaws and from the trap of investment news, which reports what has happened, not what will occur. It is out of date when you see it.

Have discipline! You have done the hard work. You have set your investment goal and decided to fund your option income portfolio. By applying the principles we have laid out, you can construct a basic financial goal and generate a plan for attacking it.

Remember: successful investing demands time plus money.

Since each of us is different, you must fine-tune and individualize your plan. You will have some successes and, undoubtedly, you will have some failures. The important thing is to remain flexible and learn from past mistakes so that you don't repeat them.

> *"The difference between a successful person and others is not a lack of strength, not a lack of knowledge, but rather is a lack of will."*
> Vincent Lombardi

Satisfactory investment results are easier to achieve than most people realize; to achieve superior results is much more difficult.

I could conclude this book by saying the best of luck to you in your stock market adventure, although we all know that the element responsible for success is much less elusive and far more tangible than anything that even closely resembles luck.

Only results count. Remember that time is your most important ally. An individual mistake here or there won't sink your ship, but you will never reach your destination if you do not leave the dock.

You earn your money the hard way, and you have a safe, methodical way of investing—and a solid foundation for building your wealth. You now have the knowledge to strip the mystique from investing. You now have a clear method and a degree of sophistication on a par with the "pros" in the business. On the way you learned to avoid the traps that constantly frustrate others who attempt to make a fortune in the stock market.

It's time to begin investing without fear!

"Don't gamble! Take all savings and buy some good stock and hold it till it goes up, and then sell it. If it don't go up, don't buy it."
Will Rogers

"The one who shoots best may sometimes miss the mark; but the one that shoots not at all can never hit it."
Owen Felltham

Stock Quote Conversion Table

1/32				.03125
2/32	1/16			.06250
3/32				.09375
4/32	2/16	1/8		.12500
5/32				.15625
6/32	3/16			.18750
7/32				.21875
8/32	4/16	2/8	1/4	.25000
9/32				.28125
10/32	5/16			.31250
11/32				.34375
12/32	6/16	3/8		.37500
13/32				.40625
14/32	7/16			.43750
15/32				.46875
16/32	8/16	4/8	1/2	.50000
17/32				.53125
18/32	9/16			.56250
19/32				.59375
20/32	10/16	5/8		.62500
21/32				.65625
22/32	11/16			.68750
23/32				.71875
24/32	12/16	6/8	3/4	.75000
25/32				.78125
26/32	13/16			.81250
27/32				.84375
28/32	14/16	7/8		.87500
29/32				.90625
30/32	15/16			.93750
31/32				.96875

APPENDIX *II*

For More
Option Information

American Stock Exchange, Derivative Securities
86 Trinity Place, New York, NY 10006
1-800-THE-AMEX

Chicago Board Options Exchange
LaSalle at Van Buren, Chicago, IL 60605
1-800-OPTIONS

New York Stock Exchange, Options Products
11 Wall Street, New York, NY 10005
1-800-692-6973

The Options Clearing Corporation
440 South LaSalle Street, Suite 2400
Chicago, IL 60605
1-800-537-4258

Bibliography

There is a wealth of information written about stocks and options. The following list contains the books that I have found the most timeless and useful. There are two categories, general investing information and in-depth studies of options.

General Investing

Cohen, Jerome B. and Zinbarg, Edward D. *Investment Analysis and Portfolio Management*. Homewood, IL: Dow Jones-Irwin, 1967.

Engel, Louis, and Brendan Boyd. *How to Buy Stocks*. 7th ed. New York: Bantam Books, 1983.

Goldenberg, Susan. *Trading Inside the World's Leading Stock Exchanges*. San Diego: Harcourt Brace Janovich, 1986.

Graham, Benjamin. *The Intelligent Investor*. 4th ed. New York: Harper & Row Publishers, 1973.

Graham, Benjamin, Dodd, David L., and Cottle, Sidney. *Security Analysis*. 4th ed. New York: McGraw Hill Book Co., 1962.

Lefevre, Edwin. *Reminiscences Of a Stock Operator*. Larchmont, New York: American Research Council, 1923.

Little, Jeffrey B., and Rhodes, Lucien. *Understanding Wall Street*. 2nd ed. Blue Ridge Summit, PA: Tab Books Inc., 1987.

Mackay, Charles, *Extraordinary Popular Delusions and the Madness of Crowds*. New York: Farrar, Strauss and Giroux, 1932. Originally published, London: Richard Beutley, 1841.

Scott, David L. *Wall Street Words*. Boston, MA: Houghton Mifflin Company, 1988.

Weinstein, Stan. *Secrets for Profiting in Bull and Bear Markets*. Homewood, IL: Dow Jones-Irwin, 1988.

Options

Angell, George. *Sure Thing Options Trading*. Garden City, NY: Doubleday, 1983.

Ansbacher, Max G. *The New Options Market*. 2nd ed. New York: Walker & Co., 1979.

Gastineau, Gary L. *The Options Manual*. 3rd ed. New York: McGraw-Hill, 1988.

Smith, Courtney. *Option Strategies*. New York: John Wiley & Sons, 1987.

Trester, Kenneth R. *The Compleat Option Player*. 3rd ed. Huntington Beach, CA: Investrek Publishing, 1983.

The Options Institute. *Options: Essential Concepts and Trading Strategies*. Homewood, IL: Business One-Irwin, Dow Jones, 1990.

Walker, Joseph A. *How the Options Markets Work*. New York: The New York Institute of Finance, 1991.

Yates, James W. *The Options Strategy Spectrum*. Homewood, IL: Dow Jones-Irwin, 1987.

Index

Investing tools that help you . .

Finding Winners Among Depressed and Low-Priced Stocks

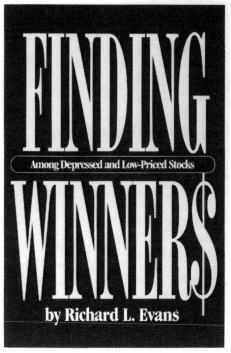

"Low-priced stock investing is one of the most profitable, yet least followed investment areas. I thought this book was excellent, and it provides superb, common sense information that any sensible investor who does not want to be part of the 'crowd' should have. As editor of *Investors Intelligence* and a stock market participant for almost forty years, I know people 'love' stocks that are popular, and 'hate' stocks that are unpopular, and that is why they do not do as well as they should in the stock market. Insights and examples found in this book will be very rewarding to those who listen. It is one of the best books that I have read in a long time."

Michael Burke, Editor
Investors Intelligence

"For the individual investor seeking large profits from small-priced stocks, there's no better guide than Richard Evans. *Finding Winners* solidifies Mr. Evans' position as a recognized leader in the investment advisory business."

Steve Halpern, Editor Publisher
Dick Davis Digest

Year in, year out, the best stock market gains come from low-priced stocks, stocks selling under $20, often less than $10, and sometimes under $5. Wall Street conditions the investor to buy high-priced stocks, but the best returns invariably arise from low-priced and depressed stocks.

In *Finding Winners Among Depressed and Low-Priced Stocks* Richard L. Evans delineates the characteristics of the type of stock most likely to be big winners and develops a system that tells investors when and how to buy them.

Richard L. Evans, a Registered Investment Advisor and the principal of Richard L. Evans Investments, is a manager of individual investment and retirement portfolios. Evans is a graduate of Northwestern University's prestigious Kellogg Graduate School of Management, a recognized Dow Theorist, and formerly President, Chief Market Strategist, Director of Research, and owner of *Dow Theory Forecasts*, one of the best-known investment letters.

To order, call 1-800-488-4149, or mail in coupon on facing page.

. . . Find the Winners

Finding Winners - A Videotape Presentation

This video presentation of *Finding Winners* further documents the profits to be made by investing in low-priced and depressed stocks. As in his book, *Finding Winners Among Depressed and Low-Priced Stocks,* Evans uses additional real-life case examples to present technical analysis in action so that investors can find the winners.

This information-packed presentation explains how to identify and use the three market trends, resistance levels, self-correcting trends and important highs to find winners. Plus, Evans illustrates how to find buying opportunities as a stock is . . .

- breaking out of a channel
- rising off the bottom
- opposing a group trend

and how to avoid some of the risk by
- investing in value
- investing in group trends
- applying the three-steps-and-a-stumble rule

A Videotape Presentation

FINDING

Among Depressed and Low-Priced Stock$

WINNER$

with Richard L. Evans

Buy low, sell high? This video will provide investors with the "muscle memory" to develop the technical skills necessary to find winners among depressed and low-priced stocks. Only $49.95 for a 68-minute standard VHS cassette.

To order, use the coupon below or call 1-800-488-4149

Value Averaging Can Help You Earn Higher Investment Returns with Lower Costs

Now in its second edition, revised, and made even more practical than before, *Value Averaging: The Safe and Easy Strategy for Higher Investment Returns:*

- shows you how to make the buying and selling of investments nearly automatic, relieving you of emotional anxiety and the need for market-timing and stock picking skills;
- recommends investments best suited for value averaging;
- tells you how to build real wealth easily and consistently over time;
- demonstrates how to use both dollar cost averaging and value averaging for specific investment goals, such as college tuition for your children or your own retirement.

Here's what reviewers said about the last edition:

"The latest wrinkle in automatic investing . . . Compared over time with dollar cost averaging, value averaging will always lower your total cost per share, and it will typically provide a rate or return that's about one percentage point higher . . . "
Kiplinger's Personal Finance Magazine

" 'Today's Best Way to Invest' The smartest strategy today is not to shun stock—but to add money a little at a time. . . . The most familiar such technique is dollar cost averaging. . . . But a lesser-known version called value averaging can get better results by forcing you to make an extra investment in a month when stocks are down and to invest less— or actually a little less—when stocks advance."
Money Magazine

"Value averaging takes dollar cost averaging one step further. Besides buying low, you sell shares when the markets soar."
The New York Times

Value Averaging Diskette
for the
Computerized Investor

- Save effort and your valuable time
- Get started immediately on your Value-Averaging or Dollar Cost Averaging investment program
- Test the strategies the no-fuss way

The Readjustment Spreadsheets and the Simulation Spreadsheet Formulas found in the Appendixes to Chapters 4, 5, and 7, have been constructed for you and are available now on diskette!

NOTE: To use the diskette you *must* have the following hardware and software:

System—IBM PC, XT, AT, PS/2 or compatible, MS or PC-DOS version 2 or later with 640K memory

Software—Lotus 1-2-3, Release 2 or higher

The *Value-Averaging* Diskette is **$15.00.**

To order, use the coupon below or call 1-800-488-4149.

Name_____ Address _____

City / State / Zip _____

Check Encl. Amt. _____ Visa / MC# _____ Exp _____

Signature _____ Telephone # _____

Quantity   Price   Title

_____   _____   _____   _____

Subtotal   _____

Illinois Residents add 8.75% Sales Tax   _____

Shipping/Handling via UPS, add $3.75 for lst diskette, $2 for each additional   _____

Grand Total   _____

International Publishing Corp., 625 N. Michigan, Suite 1920, Chicago, IL 60611

One-of-a-Kind Investment Information Guide

It took a seasoned financial planner a mere five minutes of leafing through this book's 400-plus pages to recognize its enormous potential value for both financial beginners and old pro's.

For her client, an admitted neophyte, *SOURCE: The Complete Guide to Investment Information, Where to Find It and How to Use It* provides a painless education in how to discover the most pertinent investment information and how to employ it — not to mention how to better understand what the financial planner and her stockbroker are talking about. For more experienced investors, it offers the one-stop convenience of up-to-date source information; as such it's a first-of-its kind tool.

SOURCE is an investment information handbook designed for students of finance and investments as well as for practical investors. *SOURCE* shows where to find information and advice on different types of investment instruments and how to read and interpret those sources. *SOURCE* breaks down the information into an overview, a look at how to choose the right type of security in each investment category, how to read related information given for each source. From the most common and accessible daily newspaper or radio report to the most sophisticated and often costly investment newsletter, no information source is overlooked.

Want to know about risk-adjusted yield, discount yield, dividend yield, current yield, beta, P/E ratio, 7-day compound yield, market indexes and averages, how to read ticker tape quotations, how to read financial statements, and how to interpret economic, industry, and company information? *SOURCE* provides the know-how. Liberally illustrated with artwork from representative information sources, *SOURCE* devotes whole chapters to key investment categories: common and preferred stocks; fixed-income securities; mutual funds; warrants, options, and futures; and tangibles such as real estate and collectibles and precious metals and coins.

SOURCE, by Jae K. Shim and Joel G. Siegel, who also co-authored the best-selling *The Vest-Pocket MBA*, is an invaluable one-of-a-kind investment decision making tool for both beginning and experienced investors.

Please send me _____ copies of the hardcover, *SOURCE: The Complete Guide to Investment Information, Where to Find It and How to Use It* at $29.95 each.

Name _____

Address _____

City/State/Zip_____

Please make checks payable to International Publishing Corporation. Add $3.75 for the 1st book, $2.00 for each additional for shipping/handling via UPS. (Illinois residents, add 8.75% sales tax.)

Payment $ _____ , or charge my VISA MasterCard # _____ Exp. _____

Signature_____

MAIL TO: International Publishing Corp, Inc., 625 N. Michigan Ave., Suite 1920, Chicago IL, 60611 or call 1-800-488-4149.
